METROPOLITAN ANTHONY (BLOOM)

Churchianity vs. Christianity

T0317257

Churchianity

vs.

Christianity

A Series of Lectures Delivered by

METROPOLITAN ANTHONY (BLOOM)

SAINT VLADIMIR'S SEMINARY PRESS
YONKERS, NEW YORK 10707
2017

Library of Congress Cataloging-in-Publication Data

Names: Bloom, Anthony, 1914–2003, author.
Title: Churchianity vs. Christianity : a series of lectures delivered by
    Metropolitan Anthony Bloom / Metropolitan Anthony Bloom.
Description: Yonkers, NY : St Vladimir's Seminary Press, 2017.
Identifiers: LCCN 2017008572 (print) | LCCN 2017010076 (ebook) |
    ISBN 9780881415865 (print) | ISBN 9780881415872 (electronic) | ISBN
    9780881415872
Subjects: LCSH: Spiritual life—Orthodox Eastern Church. | Church.
Classification: LCC BX382 .B56 2017 (print) | LCC BX382 (ebook) | DDC
    230/.19—dc23
LC record available at https://lccn.loc.gov/2017008572

Illustrations by Anna DuMoulin

COPYRIGHT © 2017

ST VLADIMIR'S SEMINARY PRESS
575 Scarsdale Road, Yonkers, NY 10707
1-800-204-2665
www.svspress.com

ISBN 978-0-88141-586-5 (paper)
ISBN 978-0-88141-587-2 (electronic)

PRINTED IN THE UNITED STATES OF AMERICA

Table of Contents

Introduction

*I*F IT COULD BE SAID THAT ORTHODOX RELIGIOUS thought in the western world was dominated by the so-called "Paris school" of theology in the first half of the twentieth century, the second half was profoundly influenced by two figures, Protopresbyter Alexander Schmemann and Metropolitan Anthony of Sourozh.

For over fifty years Metropolitan Anthony, from his arrival in Britain in 1949 until his death in 2003 was, in the words of Gerald Priestland, one of Britain's leading religious journalists, "the single most powerful Christian voice in the land."

He was born in Lausanne in 1914 on the eve of the First World War. He spent his early childhood in Russia and Persia, where his father was a diplomat. Following the Russian Revolution the family had to leave Persia, and in 1923 settled in Paris, where the future metropolitan was educated, graduating in physics, chemistry, and biology, and taking his doctorate in medicine, at the University of Paris. He was ordained to the priesthood in 1948 and sent to England to serve as Orthodox Chaplain of the Fellowship of St Alban and St Sergius. In 1950 he was appointed priest of the parish of the Moscow Patriarchate in London. He was consecrated as bishop in 1957 and archbishop in 1962, in charge of the Russian Orthodox Church in Great Britain and Ireland. In 1966 he was raised to the rank of metropolitan. He lived to see the collapse of the Soviet Union, and the resurgence of the Church in Russia. He died in London August 4, 2003, and is buried in Brompton cemetery.

On his arrival in Britain he was in charge of a small parish of some fifty or so families, many of mixed Russian and English marriages. By the end of his life he was a bishop of his own diocese with some thirty parishes and communities. From the very start of his ministry he began to give talks, first in Russian to his parish, but with time and as his English improved, he would give talks in English, not only within his parish, but as a speaker invited to an ever increasing audience, travelling widely throughout the British Isles and abroad. These talks covered a wide range of subjects, and although he always claimed not to be a theologian, they are all profoundly theological in the deepest sense. He always spoke spontaneously, even managing to convince the British Broadcasting Corporation that he could speak without a script for precisely the allotted time.

Metropolitan Anthony never wrote any books or articles, but fortunately, there were almost always people on hand who would record his talks and transcribe them. These would subsequently be produced in book form, with many publications in a wide variety of languages.

Central to almost everything he taught was an experience of the risen Christ he had as a young teenage boy. He describes this in the following way:

> The feeling I had occurs sometimes when you are walking along in the street, and suddenly you turn around because you feel someone is looking at you. While I was reading, before I reached the beginning of the third chapter [of the Gospel of Mark], I suddenly became aware that on the other side of my desk there was a Presence.

This was so striking that I had to stop reading and look up. I looked for a long time. I saw nothing, heard nothing, felt nothing with the senses. But even when I looked straight in front of me, the place where there was no one visible, I had the same intense knowledge: Christ is standing here, without a doubt.

I realized immediately: if Christ is standing here alive, that means he is the risen Christ. I know from my own personal experience that Christ is risen and that therefore everything that is said about him in the gospel is true.[1]

This revelation was akin to that of St Paul. At a young and highly impressionable age, he encountered God, and it was an encounter that absolutely transformed his entire life, and it was this encounter that defined the totality of his existence, his actions, and his thinking. It was an encounter brought about by the desperation of his need at that time in his life, and through the reading of one of the Gospels, the Gospel according to St Mark, and the total certainty and knowledge of the presence of Christ. This revelation, which totally changed the life of the young Anthony (Andrew, as he was then), was to profoundly influence him and remained the driving force behind his mission for the rest of his life. At the end of the Gospel of St Mark he read: "And Jesus said to them: 'Go into all the world and preach the good news to all creation.'" From this moment his entire life was devoted to this one message.

This book is a transcript of nine talks given by Metropolitan Anthony of Sourozh between February and June in 1990. The expression "churchianity" was coined by C. S. Lewis, and

---

[1]Quoted in Gillian Crow, *'This Holy Man': Impressions of Metropolitan Anthony* (Crestwood, NY: St Vladimir's Seminary Press, 2005), 41.

Metropolitan Anthony takes as its theme: "the difference between being a churchgoer, loving the Church, serving the Church, proclaiming the gospel—and being a Christian." The talks cover a variety of aspects of the conflict or contradiction between formal church attendance and true spiritual life.

> In the course of these talks I want us to ask ourselves: *what does the proclamation of the Creed or the profession of our faith mean?* Is it just a world outlook, one of the many possible philosophies, something that satisfies us more than another? Or is it an undertaking, and is it an experiential knowledge that *binds* us? (p. 20)

Metropolitan Anthony was frequently accused of demanding too much of his listeners. He was a "maximalist"; for him to follow Christ meant literally as in the Gospels to give up everything, to take up one's cross and follow Christ. Here he addresses the question of the tension between what we are and what is demanded of us.

> In what I have said, in the description that I have given of our shortcomings, it was quite clear that there was an ideal, an absolute standard towards which we should aim. At the same time it is obvious that none of us—indeed, not even the saints whose lives we can read—have fulfilled or do fulfill this perfection. There is always something unfulfilled, imperfect. . . .
>
> And this is a tension in which we all find ourselves. Unless we have a vision of the absolute, we cannot tend towards it. At the same time we must not despair of what we are, because we cannot judge our own condition; we can judge

only one thing: the degree to which we *long* for fulfillment, the degree to which we long to be worthy of God, worthy of love, worthy of compassion—and worthy not because of any achievement of ours, but because of the longing, the hunger, and the trust that we can give to the Lord. (pp. 39 and 43)

This book is a call to action, to a reflection on one's spiritual life. It is a timely reminder to us all of our failings as Christians, of our adherence merely to the letter of the law, guilty of the sin of *churchianity*. At the same time it is an inspiring book about our potential, about the infinite love of God which can make us fulfill our calling and to understand the true meaning of *Christianity*.

Peter Scorer

The Unfruitful Tree

*This tree stood there gloriously adorned with leaves,
telling everyone around that it was enough to come up
to it in order to find a harvest of ripe fruits.
But there was nothing but leaves.*

Churchianity and Christianity: Test of the Gospel

FEBRUARY 8, 1990

*Y*OU MAY HAVE FOUND THAT MY TITLE FOR THIS SERIES of talks is a strange one. To oppose what C. S. Lewis calls "churchianity" to Christianity, and to realize or try to understand how much of churchianity there is in us and in our midst and how imperfectly Christian we are, is a very, very important task. I have been reflecting on the difference between the two for years now, not theoretically, but looking at my own life—inner life, outer life. And it has become so clear to me that I have found, year after year, so much inspiration and joy in the life of the Church, in the words of prayers, in the structure and the depth of the services, in the writings of the spiritual fathers—and at the same time as I applauded all this, I drank all this in ... yet I remained barren. And I think that if, at the end of my life, towards the end of it, I can pass such a judgment on myself, it reflects also on many other people. I cannot be the only one about whom the Canon of Saint Andrew of Crete could say: "The Prophets have spoken in vain. The Gospel lies idle in your hands. The writings of those who were inspired by the Spirit are bearing no fruit. Here am I—barren and empty." This was said by Saint Andrew of Crete, neither by me nor any one of our contemporaries. It was his reflection upon his own life. How much more should we reflect on our own!

As I said, I have been thinking of the relation between being a churchgoer and enjoying the life of the Church, even believing in earnest what the gospel is—the message of Christ—looking at the example of Christ with a deep feeling that all this could be churchianity.

I had a dream a couple of days ago that I think epitomizes these thoughts. I dreamt that I was in Russia, and at the end of the service, as I was about to come out and to preach, the priest said to me something that I was told some twenty years ago by a very respected priest: "Please do not preach. We have had too many sermons." This came back to me in my sleep. And then (this is not what happened in reality, but it happened in my dream) I turned to this priest and said, "No, it is my role to preach, but I will . . . I will tell the truth."

And I came out and said, "I was just told that you do not want to hear one more sermon. Too many bishops, too many priests have been speaking to you, and yet, you have not seen in them an expression in life, in personality, in holiness, of what they said, and so their words appeared to you to be a lie. They were not a lie. They were the truth, spoken by people who knew it and did not live up to it, people who will be condemned, as the gospel puts it, by every word they have spoken."

"But then, have you ever thought of your own selves? How often have we heard, in the reading of the epistle, Christ's own apostles speaking to us, unfolding before us God's vision of life, telling us of the ways in which we *can* be the disciples of our Savior? How often have we heard the gospel—the Lord Jesus Christ himself invisibly standing in our midst while his words were read without a word of comment? *He* was speaking. In a sense, the priest or the deacon who reads the gospel played no role; he was only a voice. And how often have you heard people who, however unworthy of the message they delivered, were delivering a message of truth, a message that remains true despite the fact that they themselves were unworthy of the very words they were speaking?"

"And so, why not make a decision, a decision that is frightening, but which would be true? Why not make a decision that you"—this congregation to whom I was speaking—"that in your midst no epistle will be read, no gospel will be proclaimed, no sermon preached, at which the Lord's Prayer will not be sung? Because in the Lord's Prayer we proclaim that our whole-hearted will is that the name of God may shine, that his will be done, that his kingdom come, and that we undertake to cross a Rubicon, to cross from the land of death into the land of life by forgiving all those against whom we hold any grievance—because this is the absolute condition for God to forgive us. And we should decide, too, to stop proclaiming the prayers of saints whom we applaud but do not emulate, who move us emotionally but do not stir us into newness of life."

I ended my sermon by saying, "If you want to be true, both to God and to yourselves, do this. And so shall I." And then I awoke.

I think we should all think both of the words of Saint Andrew of Crete and of this presentation I have made, which is not an invention, which I have not worked out in order to teach you anything or to convey to you any thought of mine. Oh, I do not mean to say that this was a revelation to me. But somehow it came from the deep, it presented itself to me as an objective statement that condemned me. But also, though it does not condemn you, it challenges you in the same way.

———

There *is* a difference between being a churchgoer, loving the Church, serving the Church, proclaiming the gospel—and being a Christian. I do not even refer to such passages as the end of the Gospel according to Saint Mark, in which he says, "and here are the signs of a believer. They will cast out devils by my name. They will lay hands on the sick, and they will be healed. They shall drink poison and shall not be poisoned," and so forth. If we think of ourselves, and if we think of one another, indeed if we think of the whole of Christendom, who can stand the test of such a passage of the Gospel? And there are so many other passages: "I have given you an example for you to follow ... I am sending you like sheep among the wolves. ..." There are the Beatitudes. There is the Lord's Prayer. There is the Creed, which is the proclamation of a God whose nature is Love—the kind of love described by Christ when he says that no one has greater love than he who lays down his life for his neighbor, for his friends; and in a way more than this, because we can lay down only our mortal life for our friends. The Immortal One gave his immortal life for us while we were still his enemies. These are not my words, they are the words of Saint Paul.

So I want to go with you into an examination of a number of things. Let us ask ourselves what the Church is. Let us ask ourselves what we mean by proclaiming the Creed, and by adhering to and preaching the doctrine of the Church; what we mean by the services we should perform or in which we take part; what we mean by everything that is our churchmanship.

The expression *churchianity* was coined by C. S. Lewis. Isn't it a word that describes the parable of Christ—or rather, the event—in which the Lord Jesus Christ pronounced his condemnation on the barren fig tree? Had it been barren, leafless, dead, Christ would not have condemned it. He might even have spoken a word of life and brought it into newness. But this tree stood there gloriously adorned with leaves, telling everyone around that it was enough to come up to it in order to find a harvest of ripe fruits. But there was nothing but leaves. The appearance was there; of reality, there was nothing. The words spoken by Christ are frightening. He said, "there will never be a fruit on your branches until the end of the world."

The sinners who came to Christ needed salvation, indeed they were barren, but they did not hide their barrenness under any appearance. Remember the parable of the Publican and the Pharisee. The Pharisee could pride himself before God on all sorts of deeds. He was pious. He did more even than God had commanded in the law. But when he praised God, he praised him for one thing only—that God had created a man like him, and not a man like the Publican. He had covered himself, as though with leaves, with all the good deeds he could imagine—uselessly. He had learned nothing. There was appearance; he had still to learn reality. And God did not condemn him, because there was time for him. But what of us?

When I say "what of us?" it is because we have so much more than the Pharisee had. He had, indeed, a great deal, all the Old Testament—but *only* the Old Testament. We have more. We have not only the New Testament as a teaching: we have Christ, the Son of God incarnate, in our midst, as our teacher, as our companion on the way, as our Savior, as an example, as the one who can give us life.

The Publican stood on the very limit of the realm of God, because he felt he had no place in this realm. He did not hide from God the evil or the imperfection of his life. He stood there, indeed, in all truth. And because he was true, he could be received by the One who *is* the Truth. And he could go back home more forgiven than the Pharisee by him who was the Way and the Life.

Now, I want to start our examination of all this by a short reflection on what the Church is. As a necessary background, there are things in what I will say that we all know. And perhaps this is the worst of all: we know them, but what is the result of our knowledge? We know that the Church, for those who look at it from the outside, is a body of people possessed of a common faith, proclaiming the same doctrine, celebrating the same mysteries in churches like the ancient churches—bodies with bishops and clergy within a long line of apostolic succession. But this is what any outsider can see of it. We need that kind of description for people to be able to locate the Church in space, in time, in the same way we could describe the outside of a cathedral, a church, or any other place for people to be able to recognize it. But unless they *enter* into this place, whether it be a church or a museum, they will not ever understand what it is about.

And if we enter the Church, what we discover is that the Church is a strange, living organism, simultaneously and equally human and divine. The fullness of God abides in it. And also, all that is human is in it—what is fulfilled and what is in the making, what is tragic and what is already shining with glory. The fullness of God abides in it in the person of the Lord Jesus Christ, the Son of God who has become the Son of man. The fullness of God abides in it by the presence of the Holy Spirit given at Pentecost. And the fullness is in it because in Christ and in the Spirit we are *in* God. The Father of our Lord Jesus Christ is *our* Father, *our* God. But the Church is also human. And in many ways, not simply in one way, in the person of the Lord Jesus Christ we have a vision of Man: man as he is called to be, as he truly is, a human being at one with God. Less than this, man is not a human being in the full sense of the word, according to the mind of the Scriptures. Christ is the only true man because he is the only perfect man. And perfect means fulfilled, brought to perfection.

But in the Church there is also another dimension of humanity: us—imperfect, in the making. But we are imperfect in two different ways: we may be imperfect while we strive God-wards, or we may be imperfect when we turn away from God. It is not a matter of success; it is a matter of direction. Saint Ephraim of Syria says that the Church is not a body of saints, it is a crowd of repentant sinners. And by *repentant* we do not mean wailing sinners, but people who have turned God-wards and move God-wards, who may fall but will stand.

But there is also another dimension in our humanity, which is neither the tragic dimension of sin, repentance, and struggle, nor the glorious dimension of the saints. There is a dimension that is mean, that is small, that in a way is a betrayal and a renunciation—the fig tree covered with leaves and barren. We can find this dimension in ourselves if we are truly attentive and honest. I find it. And I doubt that there is any one of us in whom there is not *something* of it. It's a way in which we renounce our vocation, while we still want to remain of the Church. Christ came into the world to save the world. He has left this task, his task, to us. In the words of Doctor Moffatt in his translations of the Epistles: "We are a vanguard of heaven. Our home is heaven. And heaven is any place where God is in our midst, or where we are where He belongs." Christ told us that he has given us an example: that is, that we are not only to follow in his footsteps, but to follow his example and *be* in life what he has been, within the limitations of

19

our understanding, of our strength, or, rather, of our openness to the power of God, which is manifested even in human weakness, if this weakness is surrendered to him.

And yet what we see is that we treat the Church as a place where we can take refuge; we run away from life into the Church. We hide from life in the Church. How often it happens that instead of coming out of the Church in order to be sent "like sheep among the wolves" (I repeat this phrase because it is so real in so many countries, in so many places now), we go out, ready to run away from all danger, to hide, to refuse to face any challenge. God tells us to go out into the world for his salvation; we run back to be hidden under his cloak. And this not only in great things. I'm not speaking of martyrdom, I am speaking of our everyday life. We do not live our lives on Christ's own terms. We want God to live on ours. We want him to be our protection, our help, our safety. We almost (we do not say it of course, but our lives say it very often), we almost say to him: "Die for me. I'm afraid of dying, both for myself or for my neighbor, or even for you."

There is this dimension, which is so frightening. I do not mean to say that we must be missionaries, that we must go around the world proclaiming something. I'm speaking of *choosing* something, of taking a stand in life, of being one thing or another. In the course of these talks I want us to ask ourselves: *what does the proclamation of the Creed or the profession of our faith mean?* Is it just a world outlook, one of the many possible philosophies, something that satisfies us more than another? Or is it an undertaking, and is it an experiential knowledge that *binds* us? And the same applies to so many other things.

The way I put it may sound so sad to you. Yes, it is sad. But I do believe that the truth can save. There is no point in telling a patient that he is well and allowing him to die of his illness. There is no point in not telling a traveller that he has taken the wrong road. Each of us, we all belong simultaneously to the several aspects of the Church. We *are* of the Church; we are God's own children. Christ is not only our Savior and our God, but our brother in humanity, in prayer, in the sacraments. In the silence of our spiritual growth, our struggle, we already belong to this glory, which is the Church, which [Yuri Feodorovich] Samarin described as an organism of love, equally human and divine. We are also part of this crowd of people moving God-wards with hope, with faith, with incipient and growing love, with a degree of faithfulness, rejoicing in him, crying over ourselves, grateful for his love, that he loves us as we are. But there is in all of us—I believe (or perhaps am I slandering you and judging only from myself?)—there is also so much that is still of the Old Testament, so much that is neither repentance nor fulfillment, but rampant betrayal. In a recent retreat I mentioned a number of characters of the Old Testament who still live in us—Adam, Eve, Cain, Lamech, so many others—not in the crude form in which they are revealed to us in the Scriptures, which gives us a vision of them as God sees them, but in attenuated colors. But it is not the sinfulness, it is the fact that we close our eyes and do not want to see. It is a way in which we are satisfied with being given—living, I was about to say, as parasites of God, not as people whom he can trust and send, but as people for whom he is protection, haven, at times almost entertainment. Theology can be an intellectual entertainment.

I would like you to think of this in the way you would think of yourselves if you intended to go see a doctor because there is something that is not all right, there is a pain here, there is something that is not a fullness of life. There is weakness, there is tiredness, there is pain, there is depression, there is misery, there is fear, so many other things. How attentively we think of ourselves when we are physically ill, so as to describe it to the physician, for him to be able to understand and advise us how to come to health. And this process is a creative one, because it is a way of breaking barriers, of emerging into freedom, of renouncing passivity in order to become active, creative—to turn from death or illness into health and life.

I will end this introductory talk at this point. Do *not* take it as being the voice of pessimism. In a way it is a voice of hope, the voice of certainty that if we can see things truly, we can put them right. And I don't even say "with God's help." Of course God's help will be offered. But there is *so* much that we can do ourselves in his name, in *our* name, because of the greatness that already exists in us, because of God's own image in us, for the sake of beauty, of health, of life, of truth. So think of what I have said as an opening into a new fullness, a call to conquer.

I will go on speaking of a certain number of things that I believe God has given us, and we misuse. But I think we must also share our thoughts, discuss them. And so, after my second talk, the third one will be an open discussion. I will ask you to give thought to what I have said today, to reflect on what I will say next time. And if you can, send me written questions, so that I can think them out but also organize them, because quite often, the same problem is expressed by several people in complementary ways, and an answer to two or three questions in one can be more complete and more meaningful.

And then we'll continue. I would like you not to be frightened by the long list of talks on the board. I do not intend to devote all the time to this subject. I would like us to spend four or five meetings on it, and then we'll see. Father John [Lee] may start another series of talks, or perhaps I will continue. But I think a short, sharp series is good—perhaps only for me. Perhaps it is good for you to see me as I am, a little bit more than you do. And ask yourselves, how is it possible that, after a little bit more than seventy-five years of life, this man finds himself below zero, aware of not having begun to be a Christian.

The Moment of Faith

Saint Macarius of Egypt gives an image: that of a man lying in a small boat, in the night, with all the sky above him, gazing into its depths. . . . And then hours pass. And a moment comes when the tide goes back, and the skiff remains lying on the sand. . . . And yet, he still feels within his body—as though it was still continuing—the sense he had when the boat was on the waves.

~: 2 :~

"I Believe"

FEBRUARY 22, 1990

BEFORE I COME TO THE SUBJECT OF TODAY'S TALK, I want to say a word about some reactions I received to my previous one. The first remark I heard was that I had no right to spread gloom over us all because my role was to give encouragement and inspiration. My answer to this is that I am not attempting to spread gloom. I am attempting to dispel the darkness that wraps us, as a congregation and the Church as a whole, to dispel it by casting a ray of light, by telling the truth about our situation, in the same way a physician speaks the truth and searches for the truth so he can heal and help a person towards wholeness.

I have no doubt that there is in each of us, and in our midst, a great deal of light, and of truth, and of beauty. But I know that there is also a degree of darkness—of unfaithfulness to Christ, to the gospel, to one another, to our own selves. And it is not enough just to envisage these things when we come to confession. They must be faced singly, but also collectively—faced daringly, searchingly, in order that things should change. I ended my talk by saying that this may well be something of a way of the cross—an ascent to a point where the old man must be crucified with *all* that is unworthy, both of God and of each of us, and of the Church of God.

But we must remember that the way of the cross leads beyond the crucifixion, to the descent into hell, and beyond this to the resurrection and the glorious ascension. And so, we are not going to our execution; it is not that we are going to the place where judgment will be pronounced, and where we will have to pay for our errors. We are coming to the place of tragic healing in Christ in order to have the wholeness of Christ. All that I am doing now, I'm doing with hope, with faith, with a passionate faith in each of you and in the Church of God. I would even say that I am speaking with faith in myself—not with confidence, but knowing that if God has created each of us, called each of us into existence, into the tragic world in which we live, it is because he has faith in each of us, that he trusts us, that he hopes all things from us. And this should be enough for us to find inspiration and courage.

The second thing said to me was that it is unfair of me to undermine whatever degree of trust or respect you may have for me by exposing myself in the same words as I expose the tragedy of the Church. I do this because I believe that I am part and parcel of it. And if I speak as I do, it is because I have been trying to look deeply, honestly, into my own self, aware indeed, through the confessions I have heard through the forty and more years I have spent in your midst, of the fact that I am not alone in the wrong.

But there is a phrase, not a Christian one, but an Oriental one, a saying of Zen, that if an archer lets fly a shaft towards a target, and this shaft does not pierce his own heart, this arrow will not pierce the target either. And so whatever I can say is a shaft that hits me, and it is also an arrow that flies towards you. Some of you will receive the message, some will not. Some will hear my words as being hard sayings and unfair. To some, they may be encouragement and help. But I think a time has come for me, in the time that is left for me—maybe ten, twenty years, or a day—to sum up the best and the worst and share it with you, because I feel we are so *one*, our destinies are so deeply interwoven. And so, let us try to think together with honesty, with reverence, with compassion, and with daring—and with a desire to see the truth, and to work the truth in life.

This being said, what I want to speak about is *our* situation as Christians—in regard to the gospel, to the Creed, to the Lord's Prayer. And these are just examples, because each of these points could be analyzed a great deal more than I can do it.

The Creed and the teaching of the gospel—the revelation of God about himself, about men, about the world—can be approached in two ways. The one is barren and can bear no fruit: the gospel can be seen as a beautiful vision of what could be, a vision of things we can accept partly and partly pass by, accomplish to a certain extent and to a very great extent let go because it is beyond us. In that case the gospel appears to us as a wonderful panorama, as a vision of what could be if we lived in a world different from ours, in which both we and others would be so dissimilar from what we are.

And when we think of the Creed and the doctrine of the Church, again, far too often we think of them as though they were expressions of a knowledge possessed by others, of a knowledge which others—whoever they are, the saints of God, the divines— share with us, and which we can accept as they are, making them part of our world outlook. But is that the aim of proclaiming a creed? Is that the aim of the rich theology that resulted in the doctrine of the Church? And I'll come, if we have some time to do this today, to the Lord's Prayer also in this context.

We begin the Nicene Creed, at every liturgy, by saying "I believe." Each of us takes responsibility for saying this. We do not say *we* believe, leaving the onus of belief to others; we proclaim our *own* faith. Now what does that mean? If we think of the apostles, of the saints, it is quite clear. The apostles, when they said that they believe in Christ, were saying: "We have known him all our lives. We knew him as a child when we were children, as a neighbor when we were older; we knew him as a young man among other young men. But from the beginning, we perceived that he is different from us, that there is in him something that we did not find either in ourselves or in one another. And gradually, by being with him, we discovered who he truly was: first, our guide and our master, and later, our God—the living God become a living Man, the true God who had become true Man." And this is the message they brought to everyone around them: that God had become man, that God had come into this world, that he had united this world to himself so intimately that he bore human flesh, while the fullness of God abided in the flesh.

They spoke of his death upon the cross as an act of supreme, unthinkable, yet real solidarity with God in the face of mankind, and with man in the face of God. They spoke of the descent into hell as a conquest of all darkness, victory over sin, over Satan, and of his resurrection on the third day. And all this they knew; they knew experientially, and they could say: "I know it all, I have seen it. I have perceived it. There is no doubt in me about it."

Paul had not been among them. He had been an adversary. But when he found himself face to face with Christ, with Jesus of Nazareth crucified and alive, shining with the glory of the Godhead before him, he knew who he was, and gave his life to him, and later for him.

Whatever they said about Christ, whatever they wrote in the Gospels, whatever we can read in the Epistles, whatever tradition has brought to us, the unwritten tradition, the memory of the Church, was a living experience of theirs. They knew because they had seen, they had heard. They knew it with certainty. And so did many of the saints, who could say: "I know that God exists because I have met him. I know the resurrection because I have met Christ. And I know it, not as an event outside of me, but because having met Christ made me into a new being. I was dead, and lo, I am alive."

But this is not the situation for each of us. To what extent can we say that we *believe*? To what extent, in other words, are we entitled to proclaim the Creed? None of us would be here if, at some moment of his life, he had not touched the hem of the garment of Christ. Each of us, in one way or another, has been reached by a certainty. Oh, it may have been a moment, but it was and remains a certainty that, even if I have lost it, I have known it.

Speaking of this kind of passage, from actual experience of the moment of faith, of what the Epistle to the Hebrews calls "certainty concerning things unseen," Saint Macarius of Egypt gives an image: that of a man lying in a small boat, in the night, with all the sky above him, gazing into its depths, in the stillness of it, and in the beauty of the stars, and feeling that his boat is carried by the waves, feeling their motion, being like a child in a cradle. And then hours pass. And a moment comes when the tide goes back, and the skiff remains lying on the sand. At that moment, he does not actually sense the waves carrying his little embarkation. And yet, he still feels within his body—as though it was still continuing—the sense he had when the boat was on the waves. And then, even that fades and the morning comes, and the sky becomes bright, and he doesn't see the stars anymore; everything has changed. And yet something is there unchanged. He knows with certainty what he has experienced during the night before.

A French writer Leon Bloy has said, "Suffering passes; to have suffered, never passes away." And one can say that every experience passes, it cannot remain actual continuously. But once it is absorbed, possessed, it remains ours forever. And in that sense, each of us *must* have had, at one moment or another, an experience that made him certain, however deeply, however acutely, of the fact that he knows that God exists, he knows who Christ is—however little, however tentatively—and he can continue.

It may happen in a variety of ways. I remember a saying of Mount Athos that "no one can renounce the world and give himself completely to a life in God who has not seen on the face or in the eyes of at least one person the shining of eternal life...." We may have an inkling of what that may be from what we read of the life of Saint Seraphim, in his conversation with Motovilov, who saw him in glory; also when we imagine what it could have been when Christ healed the man born blind. He was born a blind child. He had lived all his life without ever seeing anything around him. And the first thing that he saw was the face of God incarnate and the eyes of divine Mercy and Love looking into his eyes. What an experience!

But in minor ways, it happens also at moments when we discover it on the face of the most lowly person, who at that instant, or in that period perhaps, has been touched by grace, or has become transparent, translucent to the light of God—having been deeply shaken and moved, and therefore could allow light to stream through him or through her.

There are other ways when faith can reach us. I remember a man in his forties who came here. He was an unbeliever, an active one. And when he came to this church and sat at the back because he had brought a parcel to a parishioner of ours, as he put it, he became aware of a presence that filled the place. He came back when there was no service, and he discovered that the presence was still there—real, objective, not created by the singing, the candles, the icons, the prayer of the people—a presence that was nothing but God's own. This is again a way something touched him.

And I remember a young woman, who received communion as an act of challenge to God: "My family, your priests, your Church have never been able to convey anything to me. I was baptized but you don't exist for me. Give me a sign!" She received communion, and she wrote to me, "I don't know yet whether God exists, but I know that it was not simply bread and wine that I received in communion." This was again a beginning.

There are others who read a passage from the gospel that penetrated their minds and soul in such a way, with such power, that they knew it was true. It was not born within them, it was beyond them. Saint Paul spoke of the word of God, which is like a two-edged sword that divides everything within us. And Christ said that he brought a sword that divides between darkness and light. All these are ways that some people, in a personal manner, with greater or lesser intensity, for a longer or shorter while, experienced a reality—objective, transfiguring.

But the result of such experiences never remains theirs alone. In the fact that we are all together, in the mystery of our sharing, of our communing, in prayer, in presence, or in word, or in writing, we outgrow our own experience and enter something vaster and deeper. To begin with, this experience of ours is like a spark in us. And then we discover that around us there are other people, in whom the same spark exists, but in whom this spark shines brighter, illumines things that we are unable to see because our light is too dim. And because we have a root experience, a basic experience, in common, we can begin to commune with an experience that is beyond us and outside of us, to trust another person because of what we have in common, and accept more than we know in order to commune with his own experience; and so on, from one person to another, from one age to another, from one situation to another—so that our faith becomes vast, and deep, and elaborate.

And a point comes when we reach something that is essential, perhaps without which all our knowledge of God is in vain: the moment when we realize that God remains a mystery. And by *mystery* (and I have said this more than once), I do not mean "mysterious" in the colloquial sense of the word, but one before whom we remain spellbound, one in whose presence thought, and emotion, and volition, and everything becomes immobile in an act of adoration and contemplation—what Gregory of Nyssa called the divine darkness. Not because God is dark, but because his depth is such that it is unplumbable for us. And so, whatever concrete faith we can express, a moment comes when this knowledge leads us to adoration, when knowledge is suspended and communion begins.

Now, all the creeds that we possess, all the theological statements we hold, try to express in words a knowledge possessed by those who had the deepest, the most perfect knowledge of God, but a knowledge that could be shared with others. But it is *knowledge* of God that is expressed in the creeds; it is not information about him. It is knowledge of the things and the ways of God that are expressed in doctrine and dogma, not an elaboration, intellectual and refined, about the data of Scripture. And this is why, if I say "I believe," I am being *challenged* by what I proclaim. I am being challenged and judged.

You certainly remember that in the liturgy, before we proclaim our Creed, before we say "I believe," the deacon or the priest turns to us and says, "Let us love one another, that with one mind we may confess the Father, the Son, and the Holy Spirit." And if we read the Creed attentively, the whole Creed has nothing else to say to us than this: we believe in a God who is perfect, sacrificial Love, the God who creates us, calls us into being in an act of love in order to give himself to us. But as Saint Maximus the Confessor puts it, God can do everything but one: he can force no heart to respond by love to his love. And by creating us, he accepts rejection. He accepts that his love can be refused.

This is the first move of the mystery of the cross. And then we proclaim Christ, the Son of God who came to be crucified for us, and the Holy Spirit, three persons, one sacrificial love. At the same time an exulting love, a glorious love, a love that is victory because beyond the ultimate sacrifice of self—*life*, the fullness of life triumphs!

Can we then pronounce the words of the Creed as though it was a description of the God in whom we believe? A description that speaks of him, with only one way of relating to us: we are the object of his love, the cause—I say the *cause*—and also, the object of his sacrifice. Doesn't proclaiming the Creed force us, compel us to respond? If I say in one phrase that sums up the Creed, "I believe in God who is Love," and at the same time do not respond; if I expect only that his love will be lavished on me and that I will be the recipient of it at whatever cost to God, then I have no right to recite this Creed. And this is the way the Creed challenges us every time we recite it. There is no way out of it. It is not a description of God or of the ways of God.

How can we answer? To say that we must respond to love by love is perhaps more than we can do. But we can begin, at least, to respond to love by gratitude, to be aware that the Creed says nothing else to us than, "Children, I love you with all my eternity, all my incarnation, all my life, all my death, all my resurrection, all my victory. I love you." And for us there is only one way—to look and to be grateful.

And if our gratitude grows deep, if our own gratitude can move us sufficiently—if our gratitude is not only a momentary cry and a tear and a moment when we are spellbound before the wonder of God, but instead results in a life of which God could say, "I did not create these creatures free at my own cost, I did not become man at my own cost, I did not send my Holy Spirit to quicken them at my own cost, because they have understood, and they respond"—if we can make all our life into an attempt to give God the *joy* of having been understood, then we may grow gradually into loving God.

And I can't speak of what it means because I do not know what it means. I know a little of what it means to be grateful; I can't say that I know what it means to love God—as both the Old Testament and the New teach us—"with all our minds, all our hearts, all our strength, all our being." Oh, I understand intellectually what it means, but I cannot say that I *know*. And who of us does? Who of us lives by gratitude—by a sense of wonder that leads us to be grateful in mind and heart, in will and in action, a gratitude that will not only take the whole of us and make us into true worshipers of God but also make us into his likeness?

Because if we believe in the God who has become one of us, he has become one of us so that we should become like him, not only on some sort of moral level—"I have given you an example, follow it!" No, in another way: identify with him gradually, ever deeper, so that one day, in the words of Peter the Apostle, we should "become partakers of the divine nature."

And here we are confronted with something that is very important. How do we treat the Creed? Is it a world outlook that is more satisfying than any other? Is it a shared knowledge of how God is made or what he is like? Or is it an open door to communion, change, healing, transfiguration? And who of us can say that, when we recite the Creed, this is the way we perceive it: as a revelation of something of unsurpassed beauty, a beauty that is tragic and glorious at the same time, which says to us, "This is what you are called to be!"?

And one could think of the Lord's Prayer in the same way. I want to draw your attention only to one word for the moment, in the context of which I have been speaking. We say *our* Father, and it is universally accepted that it means that we are aware that we are all a body of people, that no one can say God is *my* father and not his or hers. And this is true, but there is something infinitely more important and challenging. Do you realize? Of course you do, but have you ever paid attention to the fact that it is the Lord Jesus Christ who gives this prayer to his disciples? And when he said *our* Father, he meant *mine* and yours; not only yours among you, but *my* Father. This implies something very important: that if we speak of Christ, in his own words, as our *brother* in humanity, when we say the Lord's Prayer and say "Our Father," we are challenged to the root of our being, because it means that we can say this prayer only on Christ's own terms, not otherwise. *On Christ's own terms*—What are these terms?

I would like to come to this in our next talk. Let us keep quiet for a little while. And then let us pray together and go in peace, but a peace that is a new depth, a peace which is a serenity born of a new knowledge and a new determination never to say words of faith without accepting their implications in our life, and the fact that they call us to greatness.

The Gift of Grace

The gift of grace is like light, like fire. If we try to keep it under the bushel, hide it away from others to possess it completely, it dies out. It can be received only through longing and openness, but it remains with us only if we are prepared to share it, to let the light shine, to let the warmth reach others.

~: 3 :~

A Vision of the Absolute:
First Question Session

MARCH 8, 1990

*I*HAVE RECEIVED QUITE A NUMBER OF QUESTIONS, IN writing, in the course of the last two weeks. And so, I will attempt to answer them. Some are long, complex, some are brief and simple. I will not aim at answering all the questions tonight: I think it is more important that I should answer them as fully and intelligibly as I can; and if I do not manage to answer all of them, then our next session will again be a question session, because I think that my talks matter much less than the response they elicit in you, and the questions they bring forth.

The first question I would like to touch upon could be defined as maximalism versus the possible. In what I have said, in the description that I have given of our shortcomings, it was quite clear that there was an ideal, an absolute standard towards which we should aim. At the same time it is obvious that none of us—indeed, not even the saints whose lives we can read—have fulfilled or do fulfil this perfection. There is always something unfulfilled, imperfect. What the gospel says in general terms about the condition of the created world with regard to God applies to each of us in our inner self and in our striving towards the best. Saint John's Gospel says to us, "The light shines in the darkness, and the darkness cannot comprehend," or receive it, but neither can it quench

---

it. And in each of us, as in each community, as in the whole of Christendom, we have this tension between the light that *does* shine, and the darkness, or the twilight, which is pervaded by it to a greater or lesser extent but is not yet made into light.

And yet, I remember Bishop Alexis van der Mensbrugghe saying to me that there is one thing wonderful about the light: even when we do not see the light itself, even when we look at the smallest possible candle burning in an attic, we must realize that in the whole of the created world there is a little less darkness. With our senses, we do not perceive it, but, objectively speaking, every spark of light pervades all the darkness of the universe. And if we turn this saying of Bishop Alexis to our inner self, or to our communities, then we must realize that, yes, there is so much imperfection in us, so much that is still dark, so much that is still in the twilight. But both collectively and singly, we know that there *is* light. And we could not *know* it if we did not experience it, because we can know nothing of what we do not experience. This is true for our senses. This is also true for our inner self.

And so, when we speak of an ideal towards which we tend, when we speak of absolutes, when we say that the only real, true, and perfect Man is the Lord Jesus Christ—perfect not only in his humanity as such, but because his humanity is at one with God, with his divinity, because the fullness of the Godhead abided in the flesh in him—this is absolutely true. This is the ideal, and this is what we long for: to allow God, the divine Grace, the divine Presence, gradually to fill us. But, for one thing, we cannot measure the progress of this divine pervasion, or invasion, of us; for another, even a touch of the divine makes us *so* different, and should make us so grateful, so full of awe, not only with regard to God, but with regard to ourselves.

I remember a passage from the writings of Saint Symeon the New Theologian. He was then an old man; after communion he came back to his cell, a little hut of mud and wood. There was nothing in it except a wooden bench. He sat on it and, looking at himself, he exclaimed, "I look at these aging limbs, and I am filled with awe, because now they are filled with the presence of God! And this hut, so miserable, is wider and greater than the heavens because God is in it." He had no illusions about himself. He did not think that he was a saint or that he was already transfigured. But he knew—he knew experientially, but he knew also by faith, by the certainty of things unseen, not even perceived, but known by the total Church of God—he knew that God was *in him*.

Saint Paul, speaking of us, of our bodies, says that our bodies are the vessels of the Holy Spirit. We may well remember that we are earthen vessels, that we carry the holy things in vessels unworthy of the holiness that they contain—and yet, we can look at our bodies, and souls, and minds, and hearts, and will, and whole self with a sense of awe: God is within us.

And so, there is a tension between the absoluteness of the vision—the perfect and only true Man, Christ—and the imperfect creatures that we are. In what way then can we say that we relate to Christ? I think we relate to Christ if we are open to his action; we relate to Christ if we *long* for him; we relate to Christ if we are in motion towards him.

And this is a very important thing. There is a passage in the writings of Saint Tikhon of Zadonsk, who says, we do not reach the Kingdom of God from victory to victory; more often from defeat to defeat. But, he says, it is those people—who after each defeat, instead of sitting down to bewail their misery, *stand up* and walk—that arrive.

And when we put together this thought of Tikhon of Zadonsk and the parable of Christ about those who were called to the banquet of the king, we can see what happens to those who arrive in rags, unprepared, only longing. You remember the man who had bought a piece of land, the man who had bought five pairs of oxen, the man who had taken a bride—they all refused to come; they were fulfilled, fulfilled by what was earthly. And then the king sent his servants to collect from the byways, and the hedges, from all the recesses of his kingdom, the poor, the halt, the lame; and he called them to his banquet. They all walked, prompted by this call, indeed shepherded by the servants, possibly hesitant, afraid of coming into the presence of the king: in rags, unwashed, with a past that they probably did not even want to avow to the king. What would the face to face meeting with him be, with him who was justice, and the law, and righteousness to them? And what happened—it is not described in detail—but what happened is that they were met at the gates of the palace by the angels of God; they were taken in; and they were made ready to enter into the halls, the kingly halls. Their rags were taken away from them, they were bathed, their heads were anointed, they were clothed in decent clothes and taken into the hall. Only one proved unworthy, one who refused to be washed, and dressed, and anointed; one who probably said, "I have not come here to be groomed, I have come here to eat"—and made his way straight into the dining hall. He was thrown out. But no one else, because everyone had come with a vision of the greatness of the king, of his or her unworthiness; none of them tried to look like what they were not; they came in *truth*, as they were—and they were received in compassion and charity.

And this is a tension in which we all find ourselves. Unless we have a vision of the absolute, we cannot tend towards it. At the same time we must not despair of what we are, because we cannot judge our own condition; we can judge only one thing: the degree to which we *long* for fulfillment, the degree to which we long to be worthy of God, worthy of love, worthy of compassion—and worthy not because of any achievement of ours, but because of the longing, the hunger, and the trust that we can give to the Lord.

So that when I present—in a talk, or in confession, or in a sermon—when I present an absolute measure of what there should be, we must remember that *unless* we have the vision, we will not follow the star, but we must follow the star as we are, because it is our moving towards it, towards this goal, that will change and transform us.

And we must realize that up to the last moment it may not appear that we have attained the goal. There is a story about Saint Macarius of Egypt. When he died, one of his disciples saw his soul ascending towards heaven; and the devils had put across his path some sort of customs benches [toll houses], so that at every step he was tried for one or another sin, one or another way in which he had been unfaithful to his vocation and to his God; and he passed them one after the other. And he was already standing in the gates of paradise when the devils thought of a last way of bringing him down. They clapped their hands and cried: "Glory to thee, Macarius! Thou hast overcome us!"—hoping that at least vanity will bring him down. And he turned, and said to them: "*Not yet!*"—and walked into the realm of God.

We must realize that in the course of all our life we will not achieve this ideal. But at the same time, what matters is our motion, and we cannot judge our success. And so, it is important for us to move on, remembering what Seraphim of Sarov said: that the difference between a perishing sinner and a sinner who finds salvation is only his determination to follow the path—not the success, but the struggle.

And at times, the struggle may be more important than the success. In the lives of the saints of Kiev, of the disciples of Anthony and Theodosius of the Caves, there is a story of a priest-monk who had been put in charge of baptizing, and among those whom he was to baptize there were women. And he felt a great struggle within himself with lust. His name was John; he had been baptized under the vocable [in the name] of Saint John the Baptist; and so he turned to him in prayer and asked him to deliver him from temptations so that he could fulfill his mission with total purity. And John the Baptist said to him, "God could free you; but, if you are freed without struggle, you will lose the crown of martyrdom. It is better for you to fight, to struggle, to be in torment, but to conquer with pain and faithfulness in the name of God and for the sake of those whom you baptize." He accepted the challenge, and all his life he fought, and in the end he conquered.

And I remember Father Vladimir Theokritoff, who was my predecessor in this parish, speaking to an old man who was saying to him, "It's wonderful: with age there are so many temptations that fall off without your having had anything to do about it!" And the answer was, "Don't rejoice in that: make haste to fight with all the temptations that are left, because if they die without your killing them, you have not worked for God."

So this is the strange balance that exists between the vision of all and the imperfection that is ours.

The second question I would like to touch upon is quite different. I was asked, *In what sense is the Holy Spirit "the Comforter"?*

We must realize what the word means. In ancient languages the word has three basic meanings. The first is "the One who consoles," in the way we say that a person in grief needs comfort. The second meaning is "the One who gives strength," and the third meaning is "the One who gives joy, fulfillment." And the Holy Spirit is the Comforter in each of these three ways. As One who brings consolation, he can bring consolation to us if we are in need of the comfort *he* can give. And he can give us comfort in more than one way. You remember that Saint Paul says to us that the Holy Spirit of God speaks within us in unutterable groanings, but also at times clearly calling God himself "Abba, Father." When we are in misery, when life is hard, when true suffering comes upon us, the Holy Spirit speaks within us in prayerful groanings. It is not only our own sighs, our own cries—it is the Spirit of God who within us prays God-wards, gives to our human misery, to our human cries another dimension.

I would like to explain this, perhaps, by an analogy. In the writings of a Hebrew scholar of the twelfth century, Maimonides, there is a remarkable passage in which he describes the prayers in the Temple of Jerusalem. You know that the name of God, which is expressed in the Bible by the four letters Yod, He, Vav, He, which we read as "Jehovah" or "Yahweh," conventionally, because no one knows how it is to be read—you know that this Name of God was unknown to the people of God; only one person knew it: the High Priest. And he alone was allowed to pronounce it, but not in the hearing of people, but only in the hearing of God. And Maimonides describes the great services of the Temple, and says that, at the moment when the whole people were bringing forth their prayers, the cry of their whole life, God-wards, the High Priest bent over the banister of his balcony and whispered the holy Name, which ran like blood through the prayers of the people and gave them life, and brought these prayers, made alive through the holy Name, to the Throne of God.

This is what I mean when I say that even our human pain and suffering and misery can be quickened, made deep with a depth that is beyond the human, by the ineffable, unutterable groanings of the Spirit within us. And in that there is a soothing power, a power of peace; because we cannot touch the fringe of the divine Presence, we cannot bathe in however dim a light coming from God without something softening and changing within us. The heart of man is deep, say the Holy Scriptures; and it is dimmed, because it is so deep and broken into depths by pain and suffering that it engulfs the Presence.

There is another way in which the Holy Spirit is the consolation of the afflicted—of a certain number of afflicted, perhaps of few, perhaps of many, this is something no one can say. If we only could say like Saint Paul: "For me, life is Christ and death would be a gain; because as long as I live in the flesh, I am separated from him." His whole longing was to be with Christ whom he had met once as his God on the way to Damascus, having pursued him with his hatred in the days of his flesh. He *longed* to be with Christ. So do the saints; and indeed, so do we also, sinners, at moments of depth, of light, of serenity, when we feel of a sudden—perhaps for a very short moment—when we feel that we are on the frontier of eternity, that one step more, and fulfillment is there. And then we see that we cannot cross this line; it is too soon for us. And we come back, like orphans, saying, "Where art thou, O Lord? Why dost thou hide thy face from me? Why is it?" And then we stop because we say, "Of course, I know why: Thou art close, but I am so far!" And then the Holy Spirit speaks words of consolation to us; because he tells us, perhaps, what the Spirit said to Pascal: "You would not search for me had you not yet found me!" He says to us, "If you are so lonely with God, it means that you already know him. If you so long for him, it means that without knowing it you love him, you worship him, you see in him your fulfillment, your aim—everything you long for." In that sense—and this is a major sense in which the Holy Spirit is the Comforter who consoles—in this sense we must be sure that *whenever* longing, hunger, a deep sadness come upon us because we are so far, the Spirit, if we only listen to him, is saying, "No! Don't despair! Your very hunger, your very thirst, your very longing is a sign that you belong together with the God who so loves you."

And at that point, consolation becomes comfort in the sense of strength. If that be true, only then, however lonely I may be on earth, however *desperate* a situation may be, I will not give way, I will not be afraid! As the Psalm says: "Even if I walk in the valley of the darkness of death I shall not be afraid because thou art with me." And the Spirit says: "Be strong! Be not afraid—invisibly, the Lord is with you! Be strong with the strength of God, not with your puny human strength—this strength cannot achieve things eternal! But you are strong with another strength."

Although at times God entrusts us with a fight. God trusts us enough to allow us to fight without being aware of his presence. In the life of Saint Anthony the Great there is a story of his many temptations. One day, or over a period, he had fought, and fought, and fought, and in the end he lay prone on the earth, exhausted but having conquered. And then Christ appeared to him. Anthony looked at him, unable even to stand up or to kneel before his Lord, and said, "O Lord! Where were you when I needed you so much!?" And the Lord said, "I was standing invisibly at thy side, ready to intervene, had you given way."

And lastly: the One who gives joy. If what I have said previously is true, then how deep our joy can be in the Spirit and through him! He is the One who comforts us in our loneliness, who gives us strength in our trials, who assures us by his presence that *nothing* can separate us from the love of God. And in these various ways he is the Comforter, the Paraclete. He is also, putting all this together, our Advocate, the one who from within us speaks to God and says, "He is orphaned—do not abandon him! He is frail and struggling—give him thy grace that deploys itself in weakness! Give him joy, because unknowingly, or knowingly, he calls thee 'Abba, Father.'"

There is a third question, about the love of God. Can we say that we love God, or can we say, should we say, that we must recognize that we do not love him? Both are true; we love him with *all* within us that is capable of loving; and our love is undermined, anemic, frail because we are still frail and unfulfilled. Both are true. We can say in all honesty: "There is no one I love as I love God; I love him with all my mind, and all my heart, and all myself"—but we must say: "Yet, so imperfectly! I look God-wards, and I see him as though I were looking through a darkened glass, the way one looks at the sun when one wishes to observe an eclipse, not to be blinded by the light." At times one looks God-wards, and for some reason, in this darkened glass, one sees one's own reflection. Instead of seeing through, one looks into a mirror. At such moments one must not despair; one must say, "Yes! I don't see the Living God, I see an icon, an icon that I can't even recognize as such, an icon that I cannot decipher, an icon so damaged, so darkened"—and yet, it is a vision. It is a vision of the incarnation, because *each of us* who is united with Christ through baptism, who has become *a real limb* of the ever-extending, complex, multiple body of Christ. Each of us is a vision of Christ—darkened, at times unrecognizable to our own eyes, or to the eyes of those who have lost sight of the vision—but it is there.

On the other hand, if we truly loved God we would be concerned with what is his concern. When we love a person we wish to be with this person. When we love a person we want to give joy, and we try to live in such a way that we do not dishonor our friendship. Can I, or can we, say that this is the way we love God? Aren't there so many things that keep us prisoners, attachments that tie us down? Remember the young man who came to Christ and wanted to follow him: Christ said to him, "Leave behind everything and come with me!" It didn't mean, I believe, only his material riches, but his *attachment* to these things. Saint Paul said, "I have learned to live in wealth and in poverty"—he was as free a man whether he was rich or poor, but not so the young man. He was not free to follow Christ.

In that sense we are not free either. And in that sense we cannot say that we love him with all there is of us, although it is at the same time true that we do. And so, we can say about loving God what the father of the lunatic boy said about believing: "I believe, Lord—help my unbelief!" I love the Lord, and yet, I fall so short even of my own loving, so short.

And so, both things are true. We can say honestly, "Yes, I love God." At the same time with the same honesty we can say, "And yet, I don't love him."

And again, it is the same problem of the total, perfect vision versus the reality, and I am not saying the *sad* reality, because reality is not sad, provided we are in the making of it; it is sad indeed if we become static. If we are imperfect but in progress—it is all right; if we stop, become immobile, then, know that something has gone wrong.

And so it is with the love of God.

Also, a question about grace: *Is grace a pure gift?* What is the gratuity of grace? Is it that God gives grace to the one and refuses it to the other? Or is it that we can deserve the gift of grace?

On the one hand, grace is a gift, in the sense that we have no claim on it. In the same way love is a gift, we have no claim on it. It's a gift that we can receive on our knees, a gift that is a wonder. And yet, although it is totally undeserved in the sense that it cannot be bought or forced out of a person or out of God, what is given must be received. It is not received in proportion to our virtues; it is received in proportion to our longing, to the value that we attach to the gift. Our longing opens our heart, our mind, opens wide our *life* to the gift, but this gift must be received with veneration, worshipfully, reverently. And the gift of grace is not like a present that we receive and that we can keep safe. The gift of grace is like light, like fire. If we try to keep it under the bushel, hide it away from others to possess it completely, it dies out. It can be received only through longing and openness, but it remains with us only if we are prepared to share it, to let the light shine, to let the warmth reach others. This gift is *always* offered, but it is not always longed for, not always received. Also at times it frightens us, because love divine, when it reaches us, does not claim *us* as its possession. It says to us: "All that I have given you, all that you have received—let others possess. Feed the soul of the hungry." These are God's words to Isaiah.

And so grace is gratuitously given. It must be shared with the same gratuity, the same generosity that God shows in giving it.

The Judgment of God

It's a question about the judgment of God, the possibility of salvation, and also the possibility of damnation. . . . This question was born quite naturally from a number of passages of Holy Scripture that were read . . . first of all, the parable of sheep and goats. . . .

~: 4 :~

The Judgment of God:
Second Question Session

MARCH 22, 1990

T HE FIRST QUESTION THAT I WOULD LIKE TO TOUCH ON is a very big one, and one that cannot be answered with great simplicity. It is a question about the judgment of God, the possibility of salvation, and also the possibility of damnation, of being condemned, rejected, becoming an outsider to the things of God, and therefore to *all* creation—human and cosmic. This question was born quite naturally from a number of passages of Holy Scripture that were read, which I quoted in the course of the weeks of preparation: first of all, the parable of sheep and goats; then the words of Christ that unless we forgive one another, we shall not be forgiven; and again, the Lord's prayer, "Forgive as we forgive," the words in another passage that judgment will be without mercy to those who have shown no mercy; not to speak of a number of other passages in the Epistles.

This sets the tone in a tragic way; and I think it is worth coming back again and again to this theme, to find a balance. Because if there was *nothing* in the gospel but passages such as these we could consider ourselves as condemned each and all, because who can say that in the course of his life he has shown mercy with all his heart, and all his life? Who of us can say that he forgives those who have trespassed against him, or her? We do it in intention, we do it at times for a moment or for a longer while; and then something happens, and all the resentment, the bitterness, and the rejection well up in us as though we had never forgiven. And if we think, at the best moments of our life, "Have I forgiven him, or her?"—even people who have offended, or who we imagine have offended us ages and ages ago—we discover that, no, we wish them well, we wish God to forgive them, but there is still not only a scar but a wound in us.

On the other hand, we must be aware not only of other passages of the gospel, but of the whole gospel, of the Good News that the gospel proclaims: that God has become man to redeem, to save, all those who will turn to him, and in more than one passage of the Scriptures one has a clear intimation that he has come to save *everyone*. Hasn't he said that it is not those who are healthy but those who are sick who need a healer? Don't we find so many passages in which forgiveness seems to be—indeed is—granted freely, gratuitously, as a grace, passages that show to us that a person can change only in response to forgiveness as part of gratitude.

And so we are between a variety of passages and situations: the certainty that God has become man to save us, to save us without distinction, all of us—as Paul puts it, "He has come to us while we were his enemies to save us"—but what about us being unworthy friends? Is it possible that then salvation is *farther* from us? No, it cannot be. And then there is the question of justice: Can justice be set aside for the sake of mercy without any more reason than because God is merciful? Can we be forgiven everything simply because God is love? Is it thinkable? Centuries back, Saint Gregory of Nyssa, feeling that it is impossible that the God whom he knew, whom he knew as a God of triumphant love, of exulting life, should ultimately reject and condemn his people—the people whom he had created, loved into existence, to whom he had revealed the depth of creation, the depth of their souls, and even his own presence and depth—that it wasn't possible that he should condemn, or reject them. He preached universal salvation. But his teaching was not accepted by the Church *on his terms*. And I think it is important to think that it was not on his terms that it was rejected. Because his terms were, and I have mentioned them already, that a God of love cannot reject anyone. But as I have tried to convey to you on more than one occasion, it is not enough to be loved, it is not enough to be forgiven, it is not enough to be *offered* any gift: we must accept and receive forgiveness, love, mercy. We cannot be forgiven if we reject forgiveness. We cannot be transformed and transfigured by love if we reject love. And so, what Saint Gregory of Nyssa experienced may well be true, but the way he expressed it, no, could not be accepted.

All this seems to be far from the question which is asked. It isn't. It is at the very core and heart of it. Judgment is a certainty. Judgment as an act in which good and evil, darkness and light, are discerned and separated from one another: it is a crisis. It is a moment when the twilight in which we live gives place to a clear-cut difference between light and darkness. But what then is the situation? What *can* happen then?

I remember having spoken once to Father Lev Gillet about this subject of redemption, of my passionate certainty that in the end no one will perish, and he said to me that he agreed with me, but that we had no right to call this a certainty of faith, in the sense that we could not simply found it on the words of the Scripture, give formal evidence for it. But that we could daringly, with joy, humbly, proclaim it as a certainty of hope, that the God whom we *know*, however little, but whom we know, is not a God that has created anything that it may perish afterwards. And Isaiah said that very clearly.

How do we then stand with this subject of judgment, of condemnation? May I suggest a few images which are not particularly theological or elevated, but which I think are adequate for what I want to convey? If after our death we stand before the face of God, and we see his unsurpassed beauty, his holiness, and if we see him as life-giving Love, we may well shudder in horror at the thought, indeed, at the feeling, the sensation, that all of that was offered us from the beginning and we had passed it by. But can we also think that this God will simply look at us and say, "You see? You have missed your earthly opportunity; it is now too late—away from me!" Can we imagine, however high we deem justice, that any mother, any father, any friend, seeing his child or his friend of a sudden in all the horror that is invisible to us would say, "Away from me!" Wouldn't anyone of us, heartbrokenly, lovingly say, "Come! and cry.... Come and cry ... and I will try to console you over the life you have wrecked, over the past that cannot be changed or redeemed, but a past which is no longer what you cling to, because you have seen it in all its horror.... Come, cry—because I don't reject you!"

Christ is called the Faithful One in the Book of Revelation. He is the one who is ultimately faithful to all his creatures. The incarnation is an act of faithfulness. Having created us, having granted us the freedom to choose between good and evil, he takes all responsibility for his gift; he becomes man; he carries all the weight of the world. And because of this, because he becomes the universal victim, he also has power to forgive; power to forgive because he is the Son of man, and power to forgive because he is the victim of all the evil of the world. "Forgive them, Father—they do not know what they are doing." He said this about his crucifiers, those who were actually murdering him. But these words, don't they extend also to those who had pronounced iniquitous judgment against him? Do they not extend to those who had brought forth witness? Do they not extend to those who had not understood, and having received him with palm branches, a few days later shouted, "Crucify him, crucify him! He has betrayed our hope—we wanted a victorious king, we do not want a sacrificial God."

And beyond them, because he has taken upon himself *all* the sin of the world, doesn't his word reach out to all those who are prepared to receive this word? Yes, we must receive it; we cannot be forgiven or redeemed while we reject the redeemer and him who forgives. And I am not making now a statement about believing in Christ and being a Christian and passing by every other creature. But then, what *is* the judgment, the first judgment that confronts us? The vision of who we are. And in the story of sheep and goats it is so clear that God is asking us: "Have you been simply human? Unless you have been human in the simplest terms of mercy, of compassion, of charity, how can you go beyond humanity into communion with divinity itself?" He does not ask those whom he judges about the tenets of their faith. He asks them, "Have you fed the hungry? Have you visited the sick? Have you not been ashamed of recognizing in the one in prison a friend, and have you visited him?"—and so forth. The incarnation—that is, the pervasion of our humanity by God—is possible *if this is humanity*, not less than humanity. So, this is the first question, and so simple in a way, a question that can be addressed universally to the whole of mankind: have you been merciful, compassionate, human? If you have, you can *then* receive God.

And we have in the Scriptures a certain number of passages to that effect. Saint Paul says somewhere that, according to what we have built with, what we have built will survive or not. If we have built of straw or of wood, when the fire of judgment comes, all of that will be burnt. But if we have built of silver and gold, what we have built will remain. God is a devouring fire. If we are not human, if we have built of straw and wood a *semblance* of humanity, this semblance cannot resist the fire: there is something that must be burned. But if there is not, it will resist. And there is another image in the Old Testament of the way in which the fire can *touch* and not consume. It is that of the burning bush, the bush that Moses saw in the wilderness: aflame with divinity, and yet, it was not being consumed—filled with the presence of God as though it was aflame, and yet not burned to the ground. And this is what we are called to be and to become.

Now, when we think of the judgment, again in the terms of Saint Paul, we are confronted with a kind of judgment that is very different from our courts of law. Whether it is our personal confrontation with God, or whether it is the final judgment over all of mankind—and to this I will come back in a moment—the imagery of the court of law is inadequate. In a human court there is a law that is established by a legislative power, but a power that establishes the law but does not apply it. Then, there are the judges who do not work out the law but who apply it; they are submitted to the law, they are obedient to it, they are those who make law into living reality. Then there is the jury, and the culprit, and the witnesses for the defense, and the witnesses for the Crown, and the prosecution, and the defense. And we can see how it works: badly, or well, but there is a logic in it.

But when we think of the Judgment of God, what we see is that he who judges is also the Lawgiver. He, whose image—the perfect humanity that he reveals to us—is our condemnation, is also our Redeemer and our defense. And what about the witnesses? More than one spiritual writer has written that no one confronted with the divine judgment will ever have the courage, the daring, to raise his voice against a brother, a sister, because at that moment he or she will see themselves as unworthy of God and stand condemned by their own conscience. Remember the story of the woman taken in adultery, how Christ turned to the righteous Jews who wanted to stone her and said, "Let him who is without sin cast the first stone"—this is an image of what may happen: who will cast any stone?

And then, there is something else. I have said this so often that I am shy of repeating it, but our life does not end at the moment when we depart this earthly life. Of course, at that moment our body can no longer act, our soul is separated from it. But we have left a mark in the world in which we live, a mark that is indelible: every person whom we have met, every word which we have spoken, every gesture of ours, every action of ours—everything that was us or was done by us, proceeded from us, has left a trace in this world. And we cannot say that because a person has died, his responsibility, for better or worse, for good and evil, is no longer in motion, in action. Can we say for instance, that the French writer Gobineau, who is completely forgotten, who wrote in the nineteenth century a short treatise on the inequality of races, which no one reads any more, has no responsibility for the fact that he inspired Hitler in his vision of the inequality of races. He wrote his essay as an intellectual exercise—and here was a man who applied all his thoughts and went beyond them. Can we say that Gobineau is without responsibility for everything that has originated in his thought and reached others through his writings? And this will continue as long as the world stands, and as long as the problem of inequality of races, of nations, of individuals, is not solved. Can one say that he has died and therefore is free? Hardly. And at the same time we can, at the other end of the spectrum, think of the great heroes of the spirit: the saints, but also the great inspirers of mankind in philosophy, in art, in literature who have left behind thought, experience, vision which have made mankind grow, century after century, with ups and downs, through tragedies, but who have been beacons of truth and of light. They also have not ended their lives.

And this is why we can see in the Book of Revelation a passage in which we are told that a time will come, at the end of time, when time shall be no more, when nations and kingdoms will bring before the throne of God their glory—but one could also add: their shame. But it will no longer be a matter of rehearsing individual judgments, the assessment that God and each of us can make at the moment of our death when we first stand before God. It is not a question of making public individual judgments. It is a moment when the total interwovenness of all mankind, all creatures, will be revealed. And if it were not like this—and I have mentioned it already so I will not repeat that—then the very genealogy of Christ would be totally meaningless, if each of us was a separate individual and not a drop in a current of a stream. And then we will all stand as a human race before God.

But then what is our hope of redemption or our danger of condemnation?

First of all, quite a lot has been written in this century by Orthodox theologians like [Konstantin] Mochulsky and others about the meaning of the word "eternal" when it applies to the text of the Scriptures. It means two things: when we speak of God, and we say that he is eternal, we mean that he has neither beginning nor end, that he is beyond time. But when we read about things called "eternal"—eternal torment—the word used is the word that signifies a length of time. Or, if you prefer, it means *as long as time lasts so it shall be.* But when the End comes, time is no more. And the End is not a moment of time, the End is not something, it is Someone. The End—and I am contradicting myself because I have no other way of putting it—is the moment when God fills all in all, and when there is no time in the sense we know it on earth. There is a growth into God, there is a fulfillment of things, and yet, there is no longer the linear time that we know. And—several theologians have attracted the attention of believers to this—when the Scriptures speak of eternal torment, what they say is that, as long as time lasts, as long as we are *in becoming* before the final, great summing up of history, there will be pain and anguish, but a pain and anguish that is not obligatory, the result of an act of divine retribution, but the acute pain and the deep sadness that we can have when we discover that we have betrayed the hope of one who loves us with all his life and all his death, of one who gave his life for us—and we shrugged our shoulders and continued in our own ways.

So that there is this eternity, but it's an eternity that will be swallowed up by another eternity. There is a moment, in the words of Saint Irenaeus of Lyon, when the whole of mankind will become by the power of the Spirit one with Christ, so that, having become the sons of God by adoption through baptism, through faith, through our relative faithfulness to God, we will, in the Only Begotten Son become, in our togetherness, *the only begotten son*. Adoption will be left behind, sonship alone will remain, and God, in the words of Saint Paul, "shall be all in all." This is our hope, this can legitimately be our hope; and it is our joy. And it's a peculiar thing that the salvation of the world, in the end, lies in the hands of the victim—the Supreme Victim of all evil, the Lord Jesus Christ, and all the victims of history who, confronted with their own sins, will no longer be able to judge and condemn others, the victims of history who will be able to turn to God and *undo* the evil by the truly divine power of saying, "Forgive as I have forgiven."

This does not take away our responsibility from us. It does not make things easy, because to respond to love is infinitely more exacting than responding to the law. To submit to the law may be hard but possible; to love as we should is so difficult.

And Saint John Chrysostom says in one of his writings that the terrible thing is, when someone dies, that we look at the person whom we loved and say, "And yet, I have been unable to love him, love her to perfection." But then we must remember that life does not cease with death, that life continues, that for God all are alive, and that our mutual love and our mutual power to forgive go beyond the grave and beyond time. This is what Father Lev called *a certainty of hope*. It is perhaps even, to a great extent, a certainty of faith if you define faith as certainty of things unseen, and also, if our faith is grounded on what you read in the Scriptures—not only words but the image of the Living God that stands out from the Scriptures in all its glory, all its humility, all its wonder so that we must walk in life warily, trying to be worthy of what God has done by calling us into existence, by giving us life, by revealing himself to us: worthy through gratitude, worthy of the love first given, of his faith in us, of his having set so much hope in us.

And remember that no one of us will ever be saved apart from everyone else, and that we carry a total responsibility for each other. When Saint Paul says, "Carry one another's burdens and so you will fulfill the law of Christ," he points perhaps to this: we are mankind; we are more than a community—we are a living body. And this living body must grow to become the Body of Christ, and that is beyond judgment. But how *arduous* the road, how exacting the claim of our neighbor for salvation, and how great the hope of God.

Let us keep quiet for a moment, pray, and go in peace, stand before God's judgment, our own judgment; and remember that we are all in a total solidarity of salvation and condemnation. Let us forgive one another, let us accept forgiveness, and let us grow into that communion with God that will set us beyond judgment.

Our Vocation

"Our vocation is to be on earth an extension through time and space of the incarnate presence of Christ." . . . We cannot be Christ in the full sense of the word, but we can aim at thinking, feeling, willing, and living in terms of Christ.

~: 5 :~

Living in Terms of Christ

APRIL 5, 1990

*I*N THE TALK THAT I GAVE BEFORE OUR TWO QUESTION periods, I called your attention to the fact that the Creed is not simply a declaration of fact, a way of speaking about God— his creative activities, his incarnation, our salvation, the gift of the Holy Spirit, the meaning of baptism. The Creed is much more than just a statement of fact, however true—and indeed, I believe, rigorously, historically true—but the Creed is also a way in which, by asserting the things we believe, we undertake to live up to the meaning of the belief we proclaim. Before we sing or recite the Creed, the deacon or the priest says, "Let us love one another so that with one mind we may confess the Father, the Son, and the Holy Spirit, the Holy and Undivided Trinity." We can pronounce these words of the Creed about God who is love, about God who reveals himself in this very Creed as love manifold, complex, rich, glorious, tragic, saving, only if we have, however little, love for one another and love of God. And whenever we pronounce the Creed, our conscience is there to pass a judgment on ourselves.

The same applies to the celebration of the Liturgy as a whole. The Liturgy is addressed to God the Father, from end to end; and it is addressed to God the Father *in Christ*. In other words we can speak to God as we do only in terms of Christ. What we say in the liturgy is not an expression of *our* condition—it's a proclamation of Christ's own attitude to the Father.

I will put it differently: Christ is the only Celebrant of every sacrament and, supremely, of the liturgy. He stands before the Father as our Intercessor, our Savior, and he says words in which we participate. Now, this is a very severe judgment, again, on ourselves: how much are we capable, or willing, to say these words as Christ would have said them? How much—singly, and as a congregation, a community, can we stand before God and say all these things in the name of the Lord Jesus Christ himself? And "in the name" does not mean that we say words that he would say without participating in them, in the way we can read aloud someone else's letter which has nothing to do with us, which we are to convey to a third person. It means, how much do we *intend* to unite ourselves to Christ so as to be able to say these words simultaneously in his and in our own name? And not only in intention, a vague intention, but with an effort to identify through these words with the mind of Christ, to acquire what Saint Paul calls "the mind of Christ," so that we should think as Christ thinks, feel as he feels, that his will should be our will.

To use the words of Father Sergei Bulgakov, spoken many, many years ago, "Our vocation is to be on earth an extension through time and space of the incarnate presence of Christ." Are we this? And more than this: do we intend, do we *want* to be this? And do we imagine that this happens by means of our baptism, of chrismation, of taking part in the holy Eucharist if we remain passive, if these things are done *to* us, or if we do them without truly identifying with them? Of course we cannot identify with Christ completely. We cannot be Christ in the full sense of the word, but we can *aim* at thinking, feeling, willing, and living in terms of Christ.

And apart from the Creed, apart from the general tenor of the liturgy, there is another thing that I touched upon at the end of my second talk. As I said, we stand judged by the Lord's Prayer. I have spoken of the Lord's Prayer in great detail on other occasions, and I will not repeat anything of what I said about the prayer as a whole; but I want to attract your attention to something that strikes me time and again, time and again. When the apostles asked the Lord to teach them to pray, he said to them, "Pray thus: Our Father. . . ." Now, in all the literature I know—I grant you that I know a limited amount of it, but still, a certain amount of it—the "Our" is always explained as an appeal to the disciples to feel that they are one body, that they are the members, the limbs of one body, and that no one can turn to God as his Father without discovering that he is the brother of everyone else.

But there is something else in this *Our Father* that of course we have known for a while, but which we do not feel very much about. When the Lord said "Our Father," he took his disciples into the fatherhood of *his* Father, and the *Our* meant "My Father and yours: you are My brothers, we have one Father, you and I. . . ." Doesn't it involve us very deeply in what Christ is? If he could call the disciples his brethren after his resurrection, it was not simply in the terms in which we speak of other Christians as our brethren in Christ. He was saying something, I think, much more *decisive*. It was not an emotional brotherhood, a friendship that had become so great that he could call his friends *brothers* and *sisters*. It was a proclamation of the fact that he who was his Father was also theirs—of course, in a different way and to a lesser degree. We are told by Saint Paul that we are children by adoption. Yes, we are not born of God in the way in which the Only Begotten Son is born; we are integrated into this relationship of father and children through our faith in Christ, through uniting ourselves to him, through dying through baptism to everything that is not him, or his, to everything that was the cause—and not only was, but is still the cause—of his incarnation and of his crucifixion. Because still, as long as the world is not saved, tragedy has not departed from the mystery of Christ, of God. Christ *still* bears the wounds of the crucifixion, unhealed, as long as there is one sinner who needs salvation.

Our identity as the brothers and sisters of Christ, our identity as the children of God by adoption is, however, only a beginning. Saint Irenaeus—and I have quoted this passage to you—in one of his writings says that, when all things will be fulfilled—in other words, when salvation will have been *won* by God for us and wholeheartedly received by us and completely enacted by us—we will be so united to the Only Begotten Son of God by the power, the transforming, the uniting power of the Holy Spirit, that we will become, singly and in our togetherness, *the* only begotten son of God. Then adoption will have passed. Something unfathomable will happen.

But, for the moment, we are still in a state of adoption, and this adoption must be transcended by us, not only by faith, but by a faith that becomes action. A faith without works is dead. It is only by faith indeed that we know God, that we live in God, but this faith must be a power of life. It must make us live and act in accordance with him in whom we believe.

And this raises a question of all our living. To say *Our Father*, to recognize that we are prospectively the sons of the Living God, that adoption must be transcended into true sonship, means that every word of prayer, every word of the Creed must become life in us. We must *live* accordingly.

The problem existed from the very beginning. You remember how, on the way from Caesarea Philippi to Jerusalem, the Lord spoke to his disciples, foretelling his passion; and at the end he said, "and on the third day the Son of God shall rise." And James and John came up to him, asking whether on the day of his victory they could sit on his right and left hand—as though they had been completely deaf to the announcement of his passion, as though that was irrelevant, as though his role was to die so that they may live and they could reap the fruits of his Passion. *All* that he had said about the horror of Passion Week seemed to have been unheard. The only word that reached them was that he would rise again on the third day: then victory would be won, tragedy would be over—they were safe. And Christ turned to them without a word of rebuke, but with a question: "Are *you* prepared to drink my cup? Are *you* ready to be merged into my ordeal?" He took them back to Passion Week, because one does not enter into the glory of the resurrection otherwise than by the way of the cross and through Calvary. We can enter it *in Christ* if we grow to such a measure of saintliness that gradually we identify with him; but we may also enter this tragic road and reach its goal—the crucifixion, death that frees us from our sins—like the good thief, the thief that recognized that he was justly crucified while Christ was crucified against all justice, and at the hour of death asked the Lord to receive him in his kingdom.

But in order to be Christian, to be able to pronounce the words of the Creed, to say the Lord's Prayer, to participate in the Liturgy, we must at least determine—not only have a velleity, but a determination firm and clear—to live the words that we pronounce, to live our whole life on Christ's own terms. Otherwise we are only spectators of the life, of the crucifixion, of the death of Christ. We are onlookers, interested listeners who may well be moved by one thing or another, but like the barren earth or the roadside of the parable we may well receive the seed for a moment or not receive it at all—and then, however much we proclaim our faith as an objective, intellectual truth, it does not reach us.

And this is a very important thing for us to realize and to remember, because that is how we all live, more or less, except the saints, who take seriously—who have taken seriously through-out history—the things which I have just mentioned. It does not mean that we cannot find salvation without being totally heroic. But if we cannot be heroic, if we cannot act with *all* our courage, *all* our energy, *all* our love of God and faithfulness to him, we can at least be brokenhearted, be *aware*, repent.

And this is also something that is so lacking in us: because we repent, indeed, of single, individual actions, we repent of attitudes of mind, but we don't know yet, most of us, to repent with all our being for *not being* in Christ. Saint Paul said that those who have been baptized have rejected all passion, that they are carrying in their bodies the *deadness* of Christ, that in baptism we die and we rise again—we die to everything that is not Christ, we rise again clothed with Christ. Of course, it should *begin* with an act of faith, it should *begin* with a determined choice after a long testing of oneself. It should be an act that is the summit of a process, not simply a passive beginning. Our determination should be tested; our courage should be measured; we should ask ourselves questions about us, God, Christ, and the world in which we live: What do we prefer? Whom do we love more? What do we choose?

So again we stand under judgment. If we were capable of—no, if we were willing—to face judgment every time when it presents itself, we might become Christian, that is, an extension of Christ's presence on earth. People meeting us might say, as the Romans said—the pagans said—about the early Christians: What is the matter with them? Between them there is a love that we have never seen—how *is* that? No one would say that about us. Singly, we are not, in the midst of the world in which we live, the presence of Christ; and in our togetherness we are not a community of Christians. And here are two very important things.

And furthermore: how do we treat the Church to which we belong? It is to us a refuge; it is to us a place of safety. But is it our vocation to be safe? Is it that which Christ said to his disciples? He commanded them to be *in* the world but not *of* the world. He said to them that he sends them like sheep among the wolves. And we react to the disciples of Christ the way John and James reacted to Christ's crucifixion: we are so grateful to them for their sacrifice of their lives! And yet, it is to us that these words are addressed.

I began by speaking of the Lord's Prayer. Think of the first words that follow "Our Father": "Hallowed be thy name, thy kingdom come, thy will be done in earth as it is in heaven. . . ." To say "hallowed be thy name"—blessed, glorious be thy name—is not just a wish, it is not a way of prompting God to appear in glory. It is an undertaking to make the name of God holy, venerated among people, to make people whom we meet turn to God in adoration. When we say "thy kingdom come"—again, it's not a wish, it's an undertaking: the kingdom of God on earth comes where two are no longer two but one. But also, we are called to build a city of man that would be such as to be transfigured into the City of God: a city of man so deep, so spiritually vast, so holy that its first Citizen could be the only true and perfect Man—Jesus of Nazareth, the Son of God become the Son of Man. Is it that that we are aiming at? Is it our purpose in life? Is it what we are doing? Let it be in small ways, but is it our *intention*? And when we say "thy will be done"—don't we always hope that God's will coincides with ours, and then it will be easy to accept the will of God? But when circumstances, people, seem to be destroying everything we hoped for, everything we long for—are we prepared to say, "God has given, God has taken—blessed be the name of the Lord!" And in the Greek text of the Book of Job it says also, "And so, Job did not accuse God of madness." Can we bless God for the bitter things, the tragic things, as we thank him for things bright, and light, and happy?

And then again, there is this passage in Saint Paul, in which he says, "For me, life is Christ, and death would be a gain, because as long as I am alive on earth, I am separated from Christ; and yet"—he adds—"it is more expedient for you that I should live, and so I shall." Who of us can say, in the context of what I have already indicated in such a sketchy way, who of us can say that *Christ* is my life, that to be in harmony with him is the only thing that matters, that to do his will is the only desire of my heart, that to enact on earth his work of salvation is the only thing that matters to me? Who of us can say that—that he lives in me; that is, that whatever I think, I feel, I will, I do, is him at work through me. Who can say that? But of course we cannot say that and imagine that this is already reality in our life, but can we say that this is what we *want*, this is our *intention*, this is our *longing*, this is our *determination*, this is our struggle, and *fight* against ourselves—can we?

And Saint Paul's attitude to death: do we really long to leave this life because, the moment we leave it, we will be face to face with the love of our life, the Lord Jesus Christ? Can we say that honestly? Can we say that, for us, to die is not to lose our precarious, transient earthly life but it is to be clothed with eternity? And at bright, at wonderful moments when we come near to feeling this, can we then say, "Lord, let me live on earth because I am needed! I am ready to be separated for as long as you need me on earth?" Are we prepared to be orphans all our life because Christ has called us to be his presence, to be his witnesses, to be his eyes and his word and his hands in the proclamation of the truth, in enacting love, in building the City of God within the city of man?

That we are not doing it is sad, but what is particularly sad is that we are not aware of it, and we don't even do it in intention. The Church—which should be the place where we discover life, truth, beauty, meaning; the place from which we *go into the world* to bring to others what we have seen—a glimpse of it, perhaps, tasted a little; the place from which we should go forth as witnesses who would say, "I have touched the hem of his garment. I can tell you at least that with certainty. Come, come and see for yourselves!"—the Church has become to us instead a place of refuge, an infirmary. We come to it indeed infirm, but alas, we want to remain infirm, we want to be cared for, protected by God; when there is danger we run away from it to God: "Protect! Save! Defend me!" It is a place of oblivion—"Let me forget the tragedy, let me have a moment of rest." Father Sergei [Hackel] once said at a meeting, "The Church, we treat it as though we were trying to return to the womb of our mother." Isn't that tragic? We were already born, and we want to go back into the safety of oblivion, as though we are saying to God, "You want us to go out into the cold—no! You are the risen Christ—we want to reap the fruits of thy resurrection, like John and James, forgetting the cost."

We must reflect on these things. We must ask ourselves, "To what extent is my life Christ?" We must ask ourselves, "What is death to me?—my own, the death of those whom I love, the death of those who were my enemies—what is this death?" Can I say when the person *nearest* to me has died, "Blessed is the Lord?" Or is it simply an exclamation at the beginning of a service that has no meaning? Am I blessing the Lord at that moment? And we could look at every one of our services and ask ourselves: "Am I truly integrated into the service? Am I partaking in it? Or am I a spectator? Or am I only being carried by its beauty and carried away, carried *away* from all the gospel stands for?"

About this I want to speak next time.

The Tragedy Beyond the Beauty

Beyond these we must see the rough, rude cross of Calvary. . . .

Beyond the Beauty, the Tragedy

APRIL 26, 1990

*M*ANY YEARS AGO A HISTORIAN OF CHURCH ART CALLED
[Igor] Grabar wrote an essay on the architecture of the
Church, and in this essay he tried to show—and I think convinc-
ingly—that the architecture of the Church was meant to convey
to people what the world could be if it were built according to
rules of harmony, of true beauty, not seeking for aesthetics, but
for meaning. And in the same manner research has been done
about the cathedral in Chartres and it has been proved quite con-
clusively that it was built in such a way as to correspond to musi-
cal scales and harmonies, again speaking of beauty, of harmony,
as revealing what the world could and should be if we, Christians, to whom God has revealed so much about his ways and
his thoughts, tried to build a world worthy of man and worthy
of him. And again the same or a similar feeling struck me when
I first went to Russia and when, having traveled through streets
that were poor and between houses that were drab, among the
grayness of life, I walked into one of the churches and was sud-
denly confronted with unimaginable beauty—the beauty of the
structure itself, the greatness of the screen, the individual beauty
of icons, and within it the beauty of the celebration, and above
and beyond it all, the response of a crowd of people of all types,
all ages, who responded to it and were transformed, transfigured,
even for a short moment, by what they perceived.

Later they would come out of this church and walk in the streets among the drab houses, the grayness of life, with all the heaviness of their condition. But what they had experienced they could not erase from themselves, from their innermost self, because, as the French writer [Leon Bloy] has put it, "suffering passes; to have suffered never passes." And one could say, the actual experience passes away, but to have gone through an experience never passes away. We are made into other people through an experience once perceived even if we forget about it later, even if consciously we are not aware of what happened to us once upon a time. And in that sense beauty, harmony, perfection of structure are elements that give us a message, and if in the church we learned to be completely open to the message that it conveys to us, we would leave the church every time—we would leave a service, go back into our ordinary life—renewed, different; however, on one condition: that beauty should not acquire for us a value of its own; that beauty should be conducive to the understanding of meaning, consciously and beyond our conscious mind; that beauty should not be made into aesthetics. And I could illustrate, describe this sentence of mine by a remark that I heard once. Someone was saying: when confronted with an icon an unbeliever may say, "What a beautiful piece of art!," while a believer will make a sign of the cross and pray. Both would have perceived the objective beauty of the icon, but for the one this beauty would have remained exterior, it would belong to the realm of aesthetics. For the other, beauty would have brought him or her into the realm of worship and within worship to the unfathomable depth of meaning.

And this is a very important demarcation line, a point that we must be aware of in our own lives because it is so easy to be captivated by beauty and to lose its meaning. And yet as Plato has said:

"Beauty is a convincing power of truth." Unless, when confronted with the truth in any form in which it is presented to us, we can say, "How beautiful!," it has not reached our heart. It may have touched our mind, we may analytically explain why a proposition is true, but it has not made us partakers of that truth. And in that respect, whether we speak of the architecture, the icons, the music, or the form that acts of worship have in the Church, unless they reach us at the level of worship, they remain exterior to us. And the danger of all beauty in all its forms, in all the walks of life, is that it may acquire a value of its own and displace meaning, become a screen instead of being a revelation. We are told that an icon is like a window—it must remain a window.

Confronted with an icon, facing one, we may well at one moment or another examine it and admire the perfection of the work as a work of art, but at that moment we are not meeting the icon in the way in which it is intended to be met; or rather, meeting it in that way must at a certain moment cease, and all that we have received of understanding through this analytical vision of the icon must be gathered together in the understanding of the message. Unless this happens, an icon remains a work of art among so many other works of art and may be categorized as beautiful or ugly, as inspiring or totally uninspiring. And yet an icon that we may call ugly may convey to us more than the loveliness of religious paintings.

Now, this applies also to everything in the Church. Everything in the Church must convey meaning, in other words it must become transparent, must be such, or rather, must be received by us (and that requires an act of self-denial), not on the level of aesthetic emotion, but beyond it. There is a passage in the writings of Saint John Chrysostom that surprises many. He says, "If you want to pray, place yourself in front of an icon, then close your eyes and pray to the one whom the icon represents." And so often I have heard people say, "but what is the point of standing before an icon that I do not see?" The icon must have evoked a presence, and then it must disappear from our awareness, so that only the presence with all its depths, all its awesome intensity should remain before us. And again, this should apply to the music, and to the architecture, and to the action of the service. It happens, in fact, as we become more and more familiar with the sequences of a service: we are no longer arrested and surprised by its various movements.

But here again there is a danger. The danger lies in the fact that the more we are familiar with a liturgical sequence or the setting of the Liturgy or of the various services, the less we become capable of being *reached*, *hit* by them. And it is only if we train ourselves in prayer, if we learn to go beyond the words, beyond the sound, beyond everything visible, to become inwardly as silent as we can (one could call that contemplative—that is, completely open, with the eyes of our soul wide open, like the eyes of a child who looks at something in amazement), that we can receive every time the same message with a new depth, so that it unfolds itself within us evermore throughout our lives.

I remember having met many years ago an old Russian deacon, he was in his eighties. He sang alone in one of the evening services and I stood by reading from time to time or following his reading and his singing. And he read and he sang with such velocity, so fast, that I could hardly follow the text with my eyes. And when the service was over, arrogantly I said to him (I was then in my late teens): "Father Euthymius, you have stolen all the service from me by reading so fast and singing so quickly. And what is worse—you have stolen it from your own self because you could not possibly be aware of the words that you were pronouncing." And he began to cry and said to me:"Forgive me! I have forgotten that you have not yet heard these services long enough. But you know, I was born in a very poor family in a very hungry village. My parents could not keep me, I would have died of hunger. So when I was five or seven they gave me to a neighboring monastery for me to do there what I could to help and to be fed. And I never left this monastery until the revolution came. I grew there, learned to read, learned to sing. I was made a server, then a deacon, and all my life I have read and sung and heard the words of the services. And you know, with years my soul has become like a harp. When I see a word it is as though a hand had touched one of the cords and my whole soul begins to sing." So he was not reading every word as something new, he was recognizing in every word a message that made his whole being sing the praises of God. If we only could learn this!

But this cannot be easily learned. To a certain degree it can be learned if we prayed at home, if we gave a long time to prayer, if we meditated deeply on the words that we pronounce, tried to perceive their strict meaning, but also the poetry that is enclosed in them; if we became aware of the thought, but also of the imagery; if gradually every word of Scripture, every word of the services became like a hand touching our heart and making it vibrate worshipfully with awe and with joy. But all too often we do not reach this condition and then somehow we betray the services. Prayers that were wrung out of the souls of men and women at moments of agony or gushed out in song at moments of elation, of gratitude, of worship, of joy—all these words become only words, sounds often heard and, therefore, no longer interesting. If we think of the psalms and the way they were born within the experience of the psalmist, if we imagine the fifty-first Psalm [LXX 50] wrung out of the soul of David at a moment of *desperate* repentance and yet of *overwhelming* hope—because he knew the God to whom he spoke and he could hope *all* things from him—we could not read it as we do. Or if we read it coldly with our mind, we would be ashamed and hurt in our heart, in the same way in which we would be hurt if we read someone's tragic letter written from the front before the soldier's death and glanced through it with an appreciative glance thinking, "Yes, even at the hour of death this man could write well"—what a blasphemy it would be! And what a blasphemy in a way it is—perhaps, a minor one, but an ugly one—when we hear the prayers of the Church, the cries of the saints, and either find them too long, boring, many-worded, or attach our attention to nothing but the aesthetics of it—"such and such a saint writes well, such another is really poor in the choice of words and imagery." And yet, the one as the other has poured his soul into these words as best he could. And at times we can imagine a poor little phrase being said with tears, and we can imagine that God listened to these few words and saw the tears and that these tears gave a fragrance to the words, a beauty that no literary production can give.

There is a danger of being made prisoners of the beauty, and because we find it such, not to be to able to let it fill us and transform us. We may leave it outside of ourselves to be able to contemplate, to handle, to enjoy. This is not the purpose of beauty. Beauty is there to reach us and make us capable of receiving the message in a way that convinces us totally: to the extent each of us is capable of receiving the message, as completely as we can contain it, but *completely*. And this [imprisonment by beauty] is particularly hurtful in two situations. The one—and I spoke of it to Father Michael [Fortunato] and he felt much the same as I—the one is the services in Holy Week and the other is the Liturgy.

The services of Wednesday evening and Thursday, and Good Friday, and Saturday are so incredibly beautiful by their setting, by their text, by their music, and yet they may be either a revelation or a screen. And they are a screen to anyone who is not prepared to renounce himself and to see, beyond the beauty, the tragedy. The one does not undo the other, because in the sacrifice of Christ there is *unutterable* beauty, but not the aesthetic beauty that so many people visiting a church may find in the service. In the middle of the church on Thursday of Holy Week stands a crucifix. It is great and beautiful, and it reveals to us all the beauty that we are capable of expressing and of receiving of the love of God *given*, of a God who so loved us that he became one of us, lived our life, faced all the consequences of the human fall, all the ugliness of human relationships, who faced lack of understanding, misunderstanding, treacherous questions, deceit, who faced the cowardice of his closest friends, who was abandoned by them all, who faced betrayal, who faced the renunciation of Peter, who faced the rejection by a whole nation because he stood by God, and the sense, within his humanity, of the loss of God because he chose to share with men all, *all* our tragedy. We can see this culminating in two phrases: "My God, My God, why hast thou forsaken me!" and also: "Forgive, Father, they do not know what they are doing."

All that is inexpressibly beautiful, not in terms of aesthetics, but in terms of a spiritual, inner, eternal beauty. But how easy it is to look at a beautiful crucifix and not to see, in the heat of the day on a naked little hill of Palestine, a rough cross on which a young man just over thirty years of age was dying because he so loved mankind. "No one has greater love than he who gives his life for his friends." And Paul adds to this: "Few would give their lives for their friends, but God has given his life for us when we were still his enemies." Do we see, when we look at the crucifix, the crucified Christ? Or, because we know of the resurrection, can we see only, even on the cross, Christ who enters into the sleep of death?

In our days there are so many situations when similar things have occurred: people giving their lives for others, people living because others had died. When it happens, the people who were the beneficiaries of this total, ultimate sacrifice never could forget it. Their lives were transfigured, transformed. Oh, they were not saints, they did not become perfect, but they lived with the awareness that, *if that was the price someone paid for me to remain alive, I must live so as not to make nonsense of this sacrifice.* But in order to say this, we must see—*through,* as if transparent, the crucifix with its beauty, harmony, and peace—the King of Glory whose glory is humility and not power. Beyond these we must see the rough, rude cross of Calvary, the milling crowd, the insulting high priest and Pharisees, the loneliness of death, of the death of one abandoned; and the tragedy of the Mother who stood by the cross without a word of protest, giving once more her Son into the hands of God, which he would reach through the hands of men. And this applies to so many services, to so many situations.

The second situation I want to mention is the Liturgy. The Liturgy is a service that is addressed from end to end to God the Father, and it is addressed to God the Father by the Lord Jesus Christ. We *enter* into this mystery, we celebrate this mystery as it were from within our oneness and communion with Christ, in Christ and from within Christ. The assembled congregation is, as it were, to use the words of Father Sergei Bulgakov, an extension of Christ's incarnation. We can speak these words, sing, stand, pray, offer the holy offering in peace, proclaim our Creed, say the Lord's Prayer, and ultimately receive communion only in Christ because at that moment mystically we identify with Christ. The Last Day liturgy is the Last Supper.

Are we in the Last Supper? Are we aware of it? Have we come to a service that is being celebrated by the clergy in the sanctuary helped by acolytes while we are present at something that is done for our benefit, or are we the tragic body of Christ? Where are we?

And then a last thing. What happened after the Last Supper? After the Last Supper Christ went out first to the Garden of Gethsemane and then to Calvary. And he had said to us in the gospel: "I send you like sheep among the wolves." He is sending us from this holy table in the power of the Spirit, united to him in body, soul, and spirit, into the world to be his presence, to be a living message, but beyond and above all to be his real presence—as real as the presence of God in the bread and wine. Are we aware of this? Do we come to Church for *this* reason, or to be served, to be given, to find a place of shelter? One speaks so much of the gathered community. Yes, the gathered community, the community that gathers in order to receive from God a commission. But the Christian body is primarily and first of all the scattered community of people who, though scattered, remain one. When the priest breaks the bread before Communion, he says: "The Lamb of God is broken and distributed, which being ever broken, never is divided." This is what the Church is and should be.

Let us be quiet for a moment and then pray together.

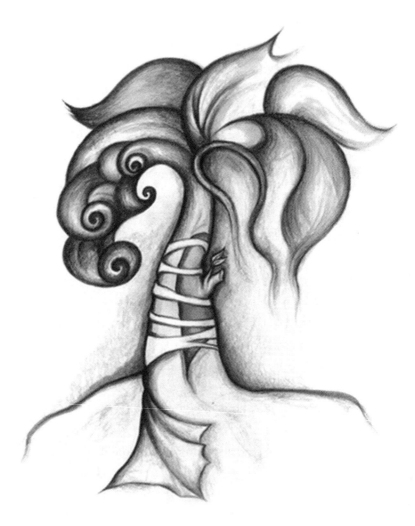

Wound to Wound

*In Saint Paul there is an image, that of the olive tree full of sap,
full of life, to which a little dying branch can be grafted. . . .
The Tree is Christ; the sap—the Spirit, perhaps. . . . If a gardener
discovers a little twig that could live, and yet is dying, he will detach
it from its roots. . . . And then, using his grafting knife, the gardener
will cut into a branch of the life-giving tree and tie the little twig
and the life-giving branch wound to wound.*

~: 7 :~

Partakers of the Divine Nature

MAY 10, 1990

IN MY TALKS I HAVE TRIED TO CONTRAST THE IDEAL THAT we pursue—and, more than this, all that is given us as an actual possibility—and what we make of it. I have concentrated on things personal, individual, on the way each of us is called to be a Christian in the fullest sense of the word—in the image of Christ—and on the way we *are*, in fact.

I want now to come to another dimension of things, because there is an old saying that there is no such thing as a single Christian. To be a Christian is to be part of the body of Christ. And when we think of ourselves collectively, we are not simply a collection of individuals, we are a very mysterious body. And it is about this body that I want to say something, and continue in the next talk, to try to understand how we can become this body *together*—not simply by becoming ourselves more holy, more Christian, but by doing it in togetherness, by a concerted effort, consciously, and at the same time carried by the grace of God. I will, as I always do, repeat things that you have heard more than once, but in this context, I believe, they are important.

If you look at the catechism, you will see that the Church is described as a body of people who are united to one another by a community of faith, by the same sacraments, by the same hierarchy, by the same commandments of Christ. And this, as far as it goes, is true. But it is a description that could be compared to that of someone explaining to a tourist how to find Saint Paul's Cathedral, or our church: it's a description of externals, because all these are things that one can study, and see, and be aware of, while one remains completely alien to what the Church *is*. It is like the walls seen from outside. But what do we see inside, what is happening inside?

When we turn to attempts at seeing what the Church is, we see a number of things in the Holy Scriptures. For one thing, the Church is defined as the House of God. It is a place where he dwells, it is a place where he is at home, it is his *home*. When we use such words in the context of our lives here, they sound symbolic, and trite. But when we think of heathen countries in the early days when the first missionaries came, or of the countries of the ancient world, and indeed of the modern world, when the Christians were persecuted, when the name of Christ was reviled, when all that he stood for and we believe of him was rejected as false, then we can realize that the Church, understood either as a building or as a company of people, was a place of refuge: God's home, the only place where he had a right to be because he was *welcome*.

There is an old Hebrew saying that God can enter everywhere provided someone opens for him a door. And in that sense, to say that the Church is God's house, God's home, God's place of refuge is a great thing, not only as far as he is concerned, but as far as we are concerned: it is given to *us* to give asylum to God, who is unwanted, or ignored, or rejected, or persecuted. And when I say *we*, I do not mean a building, I mean a community. "When two or three are gathered together," says Christ, "I am in their midst." When *two or three* are gathered in his name, he has a home on earth; otherwise, he is a pilgrim, hunted from one place to another, taken for a tramp, for a thief, for an impostor. In the Church, when two or three are gathered together, he has a home.

This is a first definition, which I believe is so important because it is so moving: it speaks of the *need* of God, and it speaks of our freedom to respond to this need. If we realize this, whether we speak of the inner depth of our own heart or of the company of people whom we are, few or many, we can see how much we matter to God: not only because he loves us all, but because we are a small remnant of people, who make it possible for him to be present in a world he has come to save. This establishes a very moving relationship between us and God, a relationship of mutuality: he is our Savior, and yet we offer him a roof, a place where he can rest, a place where he is welcome, a place where he is worshipped and loved; a place where there are people who *want* to be his disciples, and people who want to be his messengers if he chooses to send us out into the world to speak of him—to speak of man, of the greatness of man, of the vocation of man: to be as great as God. There is a remarkable passage in the writings of Angelus Silesius, who was a German mystic, in which he says, "I am as great as God, he is as small as I." This is something that relates to this idea of the Church being God's home: the *Kyriakon Doma* of which the Greeks spoke, the House of the Lord.

And then, there is the word that has given to the West the word *Eglise: Ecclesia*. In ancient Athens the "Ecclesia" was the sum total of all the citizens who had a right to vote, all the citizens who had full rights in the city. And so, to say that we are the *Ecclesia* means on the one hand—yes, because that is also one of the roots of the word—*people chosen*, but not chosen in terms of favoritism: people whom God had selected because he could *trust* them, and to whom he gives the right to be his companions.

You remember what Christ did when he chose his apostles: *he* called out of the crowd twelve men. And in a passage of the gospel he says, "It is not you that have chosen me—*I* have chosen you." They had chosen to be disciples, yes, but he had chosen them to be apostles. He had given them a function in the mystery of salvation—not of their salvation alone, but of the salvation of the world. They were full citizens—of what? Of the city of men that had acquired a new depth: a city of men into which they brought the divine dimension; a city of men that—through their presence, because they were there, because they were the doorkeepers that kept a door open for God—began to grow in depth, in width, in holiness, incipiently becoming the City of God. This is another dimension of the Church.

But who are we within these various dimensions? In the service of baptism, we are told that we die with Christ and rise with him. The symbol of the waters—apart from anything else they may mean in terms of cleansing, of purity—the symbol of waters is so clear for a human being: to be submerged into the waters means death, unless he emerges. And this is why baptism, in the ancient Church, and still in a number of churches, is performed by a total immersion. The word *baptism* in Greek refers to submersion—an experience of submersion in an element that means death. And coming out of the waters of baptism is a moment when we can breathe again, we are alive again. We were potentially dead, but now we are really alive. And it is not only a symbol, an image. It is something very real if what we *intend* is to be merged into Christ. Because, in a way, Christ is both life and death to us. That he is life, is so clear from all we read and see and hear. But he is also death, the death of the old man in us, that is, of the old man that lives out his mortality. Saint Paul says in one of his writings: "We carry in our bodies the death of Christ." Who could be more alive than Christ, in his very humanity filled with divinity? But he was dead to all that was separation from God: evil, all that was the cause of death and destruction.

And this is what we are called to experience. This is why it is so important, when an adult wishes to be baptized, for him to be aware of what is going to happen, what he undertakes. He does not undertake to join a religion by a rite—one of the many curious rites that mankind has invented—no, it is something terribly real. These waters *are* Christ, the death of Christ, and when we merge into them, we must become partakers of his *death* to everything that kills—everything that is evil, that is separation, that is brokenness—and we emerge into life clad with Christ. We emerge still, as it were, wet. The life of Christ is our clothing. One could draw a parallel and remember the words of Saint Paul, that for him to die does not consist in divesting himself of temporary life, it is to be vested, clothed, in eternity. This is what happens. Christ is our death to death, and he is life eternal sown into us, given us, not yet fulfilled, not yet realized, not yet completed—but there.

I remember Father Georges Florovsky saying to me that in baptism we become like a field in which a seed is sown, the seed of eternal life. But we are also like the gardener, or the peasant, whose calling consists in allowing this seed to grow and to bring fruit. Here our freedom comes into the picture. All is already given. Incipiently, all is received, because at the moment when we receive we do not always realize what it entails. We perceive the gift, but we do not perceive sufficiently, deeply enough, because it is impossible to perceive it—all the responsibility. It is a call to greatness, but to a greatness *so* great that we cannot even imagine it. I have quoted so often the words of Saint Peter, that we are called to become partakers of the divine nature. But can we *realize* that? We cannot realize it before we have tasted of the experience, before we have known within our body and soul, mind and heart, within our will and our whole being, that something is happening. That something is a fulfillment of our human nature of such a quality that it is not an increase, but a transfiguration.

And so, this is the beginning; and it is our freedom that comes into play afterwards. We can let the seed die, or we can look after it. We can accept the death of Christ in our whole self, but we can also shake it off at any moment, for a moment, or for a long period. It is there, it remains within us as life remains within us, but it remains dormant. A moment will come, *must* come, when it is revived. And this is our relationship with Christ. We relate to him in this strange way in which both his death *and* his life indwell us. And at the same time he accepts us within himself, because through his incarnation, in his incarnation, he has chosen to identify with us—all of us, but also each of us.

And when we think of the Church, then, in this context, we can have again another vision: Christ, true Man at the same time as true God. True Man in the sense of being real: not a mirage of a man, but a *true reality* of a man, of a human being, but also perfect, that is fulfilled. Because to be a human being in the full sense of the word, to the total extent of the word, means to be *at one* with God, to be a human being in total communion with God, in whom God dwells, and who dwells in God: Christ, the Son of God become the Son of Man, we, the sons of Adam become *in* the Only Begotten Son the sons of the Living God. Incipiently, the sons in the plural, but ultimately, when God shall be all in all, in the daring word of Saint Irenaeus, by the power of the Spirit, in the unity of Christ we are called to become *the* only son of God, the whole of mankind become *the* son of God in the Only-Begotten.

Our life begins at our birth, at our baptism. Our life begins as a sonship by adoption, and this adoption gradually melts, fades, becomes transparent until there is no adoption left—there is only sonship. I am using the word *sonship* because I have no other word, but this means daughtership/sonship, a relationship between us and God that makes us his only children, his real children, not by adoption. Although it begins in adoption, it is fulfilled in reality.

And in the Church we have Christ, who is a vision of what man is, what a human being is, but in the Church we have also ourselves, what we are. And we are, as I said in the beginning, *incipiently*, potentially, the likeness of Christ, but not yet fulfilled. *All* is given. It is for us not only to receive, but to make all that is given bear fruit in order for us to attain the full measure of the stature of Christ of which Saint Paul speaks: to grow into his measure of humanity filled with divinity.

And the Church, as far as we think of the Church in Christ, is simultaneously these two things: the perfect body in him, and the *im*perfect body in us. But imperfect in a very different sense from *alien*: imperfect in a static sense, imperfect because it is not yet come to perfection, it is not yet fulfilled, it has not reached its greatness but is in motion towards it. And here, a word of Saint Ephraim of Syria could be remembered, which I think is so important, when he says that the Church is not the assembly of those who are already saints, it is a crowd of repenting sinners—and repenting not in the sense of bewailing their sins, but of tearing themselves away from all temptation, from all evil, from all godlessness, from all self-centeredness, from all rejection of one another, and turning their face Godwards, and moving Godwards. And the condition for it—here Saint Seraphim is right when he says that the only difference between a perishing sinner and one who grows into saintliness is *determination*: it is in our hands.

And so the Church has these two polarities: on the one hand we see mankind, we see ourselves, we see the Church perfectly fulfilled in all glory in the person of Christ, and at the same time we are aware that we are still pilgrims, still on the way—and yet we *are* pilgrims. In what sense? In the sense that our City, the place to which we belong, is *in* God: the place to which we belong is the City of God, the place to which we belong is that fulfillment that we see in Christ and that relationship that there is between Christ, the Son of God, and his—*and our*—Father.

This is the Church in motion, in *becoming*—in us as already revealed in him—in a becoming in which each of us has a total responsibility not only for himself, herself, but for the whole body and the whole destiny of mankind, because if *one* perishes, the whole is *incomplete*. This is something so great, and so frightening. No one can be satisfied or at peace if he or she grows into God while another person falls away and drowns ever deeper. If *one* perishes, the whole body is lost.

You remember, probably, how Moses was commanded by God to take the people of God from Egypt into the Promised Land, and what he said to the Lord was, "If *you* do not come with us, there is no point in our going!" How wonderful, how daring a word, how beautiful a thing: if God doesn't go with us, there is no point in the pilgrimage, we are no longer pilgrims—we are tramps. It is because we have a *City*, an abiding city, as the Apostle puts it, that we can be pilgrims on earth in the sense that we do not belong to it completely, but we are *sent* into it: we are not *of* the world, yet we are *in* the world. And that gives scope both to our struggle for saintliness and, at the same time, for the awareness of the *in*completeness, *im*perfection of the total body because each of its members is incomplete; and, at the same time, of the fact that our incompleteness cannot destroy the wholeness of the Church, because the wholeness of the Church, God in man and man in God, is realized in the First-Born of the Church, in the Lord Jesus Christ.

In that sense, the incarnation was an eschatological event, and the word *eschaton* in Greek means something that is either final or decisive. Final it will be, decisive it *is* already. It has already happened, and it is still to happen. We are all already in Christ—but we must reach the full stature of Christ. The Church is still imperfect in its members, in its structures, in the quality of community that we represent, and yet, at the heart of it, there is the fullness of the divine victory.

But the Church is not only in Christ; the Church is also *alive in the Spirit*—the Holy Spirit who proceeds from the Father and is sent by the Son: the Comforter. But not only the Comforter. The Comforter would be an outsider, one who consoles us for our separation from Christ and the distance that separates us from God, our Father. The one who will give us strength to fight, the one who will give us the joy of fulfillment to the extent to which we already can experience it—this would still be an outsider. But the Holy Spirit is more intimately linked with us than this. The Lord sent us the Spirit, and we are called—and again, in the words of the Apostle, we *are*, we are not only called, we *are* the dwelling place of the Spirit. He lives in us. He lives in us, *fighting* for us—in one of the English translations, *molding* within *us* the image of Christ—speaking *within* us the words of sonship: "Abba, Father!"

And, when we are incapable of pronouncing these words of sonship consciously, still speaking *to* God in unutterable groanings, in the groanings of one who gropes, and longs, and is blind, and cannot find his way, and is in fetters, and yet who longs desperately for the *only* thing that can be his fulfillment, while he does not know what this thing is, one who feels that within himself there is a vastness that seems to be terrifying, a desert, and yet who feels that, unless this desert comes to life, he will die in it. And the Spirit teaches us this *groaning*, and revives in us the longing, and the hunger, and the thirst, makes us *indeed* to know ourselves as the parched earth longing for the dew and longing for the rain. And the same Spirit abides in each of us in the same way each of us is a living member, a living limb, of the body of Christ.

How do we relate then to Christ and the Spirit? In Saint Paul there is an image, that of the olive tree full of sap, full of life, to which a little dying branch can be grafted—a dying branch that will be grafted to this tree and live by the sap that runs in it. The Tree is Christ; the sap—the Spirit, perhaps. But when we pursue this image, we see something that is both wonderful and tragic. If a gardener discovers a little twig that *could* live, and yet is dying, he will detach it from its roots. At that moment, the ephemeral, the transitory, the precarious life that still existed in this little twig, runs out of it in drops of sap; it is death, more death than there was in the precarious life before, and a wound. And then, using his grafting knife, the gardener will cut into a branch of the life-giving tree and tie the little twig and the life-giving branch *wound to wound*. And this will allow the little twig to live by the sap of the tree. The tree will give it life, but it will not make it different from what it is; this little branch, which would have died, will not be made into what it is not. On the contrary, all its potentialities, all that it can be will be enhanced, fulfilled, brought to perfection; it will blossom out in *all* its potential glory. So are we linked with Christ: dying in baptism, that is death to death, wound to wound, and becoming alive through our communion with him. And in our terms, there is a moment when communion acquires a peculiarly great sense, mysterious and yet experientially clear to all of us to a certain extent. It is communion with the holy body and blood of Christ in the Eucharist. It is the humanity of Christ of which we become partakers, a humanity that is filled with the divinity of the Son of God. And what happens to us is so close to what happens to the bread and the wine. God fills this bread, God fills this wine, they become his body and his blood—and yet they remain bread and wine, because God, when he unites himself to the created, does not *destroy* what he has created: he fulfills it.

And in the end, the most adequate image of the Church, when it is seen in Christ and in the Spirit, is perhaps that of the burning bush, the bush that Moses saw in the desert *aflame*—aflame with the fire of God, aflame with the fire that did not consume, but assimilated the bush to him, to make the bush into a fire, and the fire one with the bush.

This is what the Church *is* in her essence, in her being. And *in* Christ and *in* the Spirit, it relates, in a way perhaps too mysterious to be spoken of, to the Father, but that is something for the age to come, when all things will be fulfilled, when all things will have come to fruition, when God shall be all in all. This is the image of what the Church is in her essence, in her nature, but also in her *becoming*, because this is going on, this is happening in each of us, in all of us. It is happening, and we are not sufficiently aware of it! We look at one another, and what do we see? We see the most habitual persons. We recognize one another, we call each other by our secular names; even our baptismal names in a way are names of history, of time. There will be a moment when each of us will *know* his or her name. The Book of Revelation speaks of it when it says that, at the end of time, each of us will receive a name that no one knows but God and he who receives him. Perhaps is it the name by which each of us is called when God creates him, calls him, loves him into existence? I do not know, but it is a name that will be *us*, totally, and we will be *it* totally.

This we can see already fulfilled in the angels of God. You know that the angels of God are many, and each of them has a name; and each of the names sums up what he represents in relation to God: "No-One Like God," "Strength of God," "God Heals," "God is Light," "Prayer to God," "Blessing of God," "Ascent into God." And if we only could see ourselves, however little, in those terms, then we could see something in ourselves so great and so holy that we would treat ourselves in a way in which we do not treat ourselves habitually.

I want to conclude by telling you a story.[1] There was once a group of monks who belonged to a formerly flourishing monastery, which had gradually died, and they were the last remnants— no one was coming. And in trouble, in worry, one of them went into the woods and met a rabbi who had a hut there, and asked for advice: how to revive this monastery, what to do about it? And the rabbi had nothing to offer, except that he said a very strange thing. He said: "There is only one thing I can tell you: one of you is the Messiah." And this monk returned to his three or four brothers

---

[1]In this talk, Met. Anthony then went on to read a story from a book on community by an American psychologist: M. Scott Peck, *The Different Drum: Community Making and Peace* (New York, NY: Touchstone, 1987), 13–15. In a later talk, however, Met. Anthonuy retold the story in his own words. It is this version of the story that is included above, in the metropolitan's own words.—*Ed.*

and told them what he had heard, and they were puzzled. They had no idea what it could mean, but they kept turning it over in their minds. Was it really true that one of them was the Messiah?! Who could it be? Could it be him, or the other, or the other? Or, they asked themselves: could it be myself? And because every one of them, including the one that was asking the question, could be the Messiah, they began to look at one another with new eyes, to see one another differently, to treat one another differently, to treat one another as though this brother or that brother could possibly be the Messiah and, therefore, deserved all the care, all the veneration, all the respect, all the service, all the love, all the forgiveness, all the forbearance, that the Messiah had a right to (although it was not only reverence and love, but also forbearance and patience, because each of them was imperfect and needed the support of the brotherhood to grow into the full measure of being the Messiah). And they began to treat themselves accordingly: "What if I am the Messiah, potentially? How worshipfully must I treat myself!" And the result was that a new relationship was established between all of them, so that people who came saw a brotherhood that they had never seen before, people who treated one another as though they were God in their midst, the Anointed One in their midst, and who behaved as though they might themselves be the Anointed One, the Christ. And gradually more people came, settled around them.

I will end my talk at this point, and leave you to meditate on the meaning of this. If we could achieve *something* of this attitude to one another, if we could begin to ask ourselves: "Is so-and-so not the messenger of God? Is he or she not, by any chance, the one who reveals Christ, God, man to me?"—we might perhaps begin to create a Christian community.

A Lone Wolf

Openness means to be vulnerable, and this can be done only if we want, desperately, to reach wholeness and integrity. . . . In the Church it is a problem that stands before us as an absolute challenge, because unless we attempt to achieve it, we have failed in becoming the Church singly and collectively. Of all people I'm probably the worst in that respect, because I'm a lone wolf by character. I have been trained to be alone to function. I am aware of that. But we must try.

~: 8 :~

"You Are My Joy!"

I N MY LAST TALK I SPOKE OF THE CHURCH AND TRIED TO give you an image of the Church as it *is* invisibly—already fulfilled, already in full glory. Because in the Church the Lord Jesus Christ, true Man, is also true God, and in him we see all things already fulfilled, we see our humanity before us in its Exemplar, in all its greatness and splendor.

We also see in his incarnation, and not only *we* see but the whole created world sees itself, all its materiality united to the Godhead in glory. And in the holy ascension of Christ we see humanity and all things created entering into the depths of the divine mystery and man sitting at the right hand of Glory. Yet, on earth, what is already given, the victory that is already won, must be assimilated step by step by every one of us from generation to generation. And in this we can also see clearly that the Church is both already fulfilled in Christ—in process of fulfillment, but *so close* to the goal in the saints of God, and at the same time so frail, so much in *becoming* in each of us and in all of us. And I think we can apply to the Church—that is, to us—the words of the gospel that the light shines in the darkness but the darkness cannot quench it, cannot put it out. Because in each of us there is this seed of life eternal, this spark of eternity, which nothing can quench, nothing can destroy, any more than the image of God imprinted in each of us can ever be undone. It is holy and it is within each of us. And so in each of us the image is already quickened, made dynamically powerful by our union with Christ through baptism, and filled again dynamically, powerfully, in the mystery of chrismation by the Holy Spirit. We are already an extension—through centuries and thousands of years, through all the space of the earth—we are already an extension of the incarnate presence of Christ. At the same time, we are not yet complete and yet already fulfilled. And there is in the Church this sort of duality: on the one hand we are right and we are within our rights to say *all* we say about the Church in its greatness, holiness, and unity with God—that it is an organism of love, that it is a unique body. And at the same time we must realize that in each of us and in us collectively it is still in motion—and not necessarily in motion towards victory, because at every moment we waver between life and death, between eternity and time, between God and darkness. And yet we can be sure of the victory.

Now, what I want to speak about in this context is not of darkness, not even of imperfection as such, but of the fact of the necessity of achieving more than we possess already, and achieving it by the grace of God, yes, but also by our own efforts. Because there is what the Greeks called a synergy, a working together between God and us, and Saint Paul already said it when he said that we are co-workers of God, and co-workers of God not only in and for the salvation of the world but in and for our own fulfillment. We must grow to the full measure of the stature of Christ. This is a command, this is not optional. Or if you prefer, it is not a command, it is a call: God saying to us, "You will never be fulfilled unless you reach that measure, and you will never reach it unless I help you. Without me you can do nothing." And again,

Saint Paul hoped for strength in order to achieve his vocation and fulfill his mission and was told that he did not need strength, that "My strength deploys itself in weakness"—not in slackness, not in cowardice, not in laziness, but in surrender, in flexibility, in transparency. And having discovered that—discovered that he is weak and that he can do nothing of himself—later Paul exclaims: "And yet all things are possible unto me in the strength of Christ who sustains me." This is our condition. Indeed we are not all of the stature of Paul, but we are all moving in the same direction as Paul. And it is so encouraging to think that the greatest need the same help as the weakest. The greatest saints up to the last moment can fail their vocation, but at no moment are they left bereft of God's help.

Those of you who were here last time may remember that I told the story of the "Rabbi's Gift." But the point is not so much about what happened as a result of this "discovery" they made, but of the use *we* can make of these thoughts. We know, we proclaim, we profess that each of us is made in the image of God, that each of us has the divine image imprinted in him, which cannot be erased. Though it can be profaned, it cannot be destroyed. We all know—because we have believed or sustained the belief that was offered us when we were still incapable of choosing, because we believe in Christ, because we were baptized *into* Christ, into his death and into his resurrection, because we have been filled with the Spirit of God in the way Christ was filled, in his humanity, when he was baptized by John in the Jordan—we know because of these things that we can both behave and treat ourselves accordingly.

Of course we *do not realize* this because it is so easy to see in each other and in ourselves how imperfect, what a distorted image we are, as though we saw one another and ourselves in a distorting mirror. You know this passage in the Gospel that if your eye is clear you can see, but if it is not clear, everything is distorted. Well, that is it. Our sight is like one of those strange curved mirrors that give a completely distorted, ridiculous, or frightening image of the person who stands in front of them. We must learn to see the Image in ourselves and in others.

And it is very important to be able to learn to see it in ourselves because if we cannot *through* the twilight, *through* the darkness, *through* the distortion, *through* the sinfulness, *through* the frailty, through all the wrong that can be in us, if we are incapable of looking deeper than that to see in ourselves the Image, we will never be able to see it in others, because the opacity is greater. There will be two opacities, as it were, to pierce: our own and that of the other person. So, when Christ says "love your neighbor as yourself," it is something absolutely central. We *must* learn to love ourselves in order to be able to love our neighbor.

But to love ourselves does not mean to wish to gratify all our whims, give way to all our desires and so forth, no, it means to look into ourselves and see this beauty that God sees in us, which is imprinted in us, and rejoice in it, and feed it, and strengthen it, and free it from fetters and give it full freedom, and support it, and in this process discover the beauty of every other person—*through*, in spite of, all that is repulsive, all that is difficult, all that we wish we could reject.

This is not an easy task. Only saints managed this. Only Seraphim of Sarov could say to *every* person who came: "My joy!" We cannot say that to one another. We can say this at times more or less fully to one or another person, but we cannot look at one another, at each other, and say, "You are my joy!" A French sister,

Elizabeth of the Trinity, in her diaries says: "Lord, I cannot spend much time in chapel, because I am busy with people. But I know that each of them is an image of you and I can worship you in each person while I am working with them." That is something we could do, if we set out to do it, if *a priori* we said: "I will meet with darkness, I will meet with imperfection, I will meet with things that repel me, [things] that I condemn with all the fibers of my heart, and yet I will believe that beyond this there is the hidden image." Saint Ephrem of Syria, in one of his writings, says that the whole kingdom of God is at the core of each person. God places it there when he creates each one of us, and the purpose of one's life is to dig and dig into the depths until we reach this point where the treasure is hidden. This applies to each of us but it also applies to us in relation to others. And this is the only way we can, however incipiently, however imperfectly but with true reality, try to create a community of people that is not a mockery—a mockery against the very notion of community and against the Church, which is community, a community vaster than we are, because God is intrinsic to it. It is a body simultaneously and equally human and divine in Christ, in the Spirit, in the Father, and incipiently already in us.

Those of you who have read or begun to read *The Different Drum* will have discovered that Peck points to the building of a community, how one can do it when it does not exist. He says that, to begin with, every community of people, every assembly of people, is a pseudo-community, a false community. I will not repeat his argument without comments so do not take it as quotations from him. The mistakes are mine and the thoughts are his.

A community is defined by having something in common. What do we have in common? We have our God and our faith in common, which is certainty about things unseen. But this certainty about things unseen, as I said a moment ago, should extend to the image of God in each of us. We also have in common God's call to become not only an assemblage of people, but to become a Body, a living Body, so that each of us perceives the other as a limb of a body to which he belongs as another limb. And Paul says, "If one limb suffers the whole body suffers." We know this when we suffer physically or mentally. So here is a problem for us. We have all that, but what do we make of it and why? We are not a community in the full sense of the word, because what we have is an objective knowledge: things are objectively there, but subjectively they do not affect us sufficiently, with completeness.

We live within a world, but we do not integrate it to our spiritual experience. We do not even integrate our neighbor into it: there is no such thing. And why? Partly because we are used to glib relationships that present no danger to either party. We have learned, all of us, the whole of humanity, except at moments of crisis and violence, we have all learned that if we avoid speaking bluntly, telling the truth as it is, if we learn enough ways to avoid hurting each other—and even more, if we learn to move between rocks so as never to be hurt ourselves—we can have such smooth, painless relationships with one another. And these painless relationships allow us to be quite happy with one another until we discover that we are in a state of crisis. And then we see that the way in which we have been relating to others does not allow us now to relate with such completeness as to be helped—and vice versa, if necessary, to help another. Fear of being hurt, fear of being exposed, fear of being known, prevents us from opening ourselves but also from accepting that another person should open herself to us, because it is frightening. I have seen it so often and so much, and so painfully when people come to visit the sick, a dying person, for instance, or a person who will die eventually and who is in a hospital bed, and one can see and perceive the fear in the visitor: "How shall I cope, how shall I face it, how shall I relate so as not to hurt and not to be involved definitively in something I cannot face?" And so often I have heard the visitor say: "How are you today?" And seeing the expression of the eyes, the tentative, frightened tone of voice, the sick person says: "Thank you, quite well in fact." It is untrue, but it is the response to the untruth within the question. And then the other person, out of fear and with the joy of being let off, would say, "Oh, I'm so happy that you feel better." And this is the end. There will never be any help received or given.

This is something that affects so many of our relationships in the whole world indeed, but it is particularly painful and untrue in the Church, which is *meant* to be a place of mutual trust, of the kind of love that is described by Christ in the gospel and so forth. What is it that prevents us from being open? It's the fear of being wounded, the fear of being seen as we are, instead of presenting an image of what we are. And at times to be seen as we are is the only way in which we can place ourselves in such a situation that we can begin to change freely, daringly, joyfully, because there is nothing to hide anymore.

I remember a man in prison. I used to visit Wandsworth prison quite a lot, and one of the men who was there, an Orthodox, said to me: "I am so happy I have been found out, arrested, put into prison." And I said to him with great surprise: "What are you happy about?" And he said: "I was a professional thief, but I realized how wrong I was. But whenever I tried to change my ways, I saw that people looked at me with suspicion: 'What is wrong with him that he is becoming different from what he was or from the man we knew or thought he was?' And so I did not dare change radically because it would have exposed me and I was afraid of it. And then I was caught. And people looked and said: 'Oh, so that is what he was, that is what he is, and perhaps his efforts to do something different were his attempts at changing.' And instead of simple rejection, people looked at me," he said, "with curiosity. I was not simply a thief; I was a thief with a problem." And he said, "I will do my time in prison, three years, and then I will go back to the same place, but I can change radically: I have no reason to hide anything." And so often it would be such a help if we could do that, perhaps not to a whole community, because we are not ready for it, we are not mature enough for it, but at least with regard to a small group of people—two or three gathered together in God's name, in whose midst we could say: "Look, that is what I am, can you carry me or not?"

You know, the early Church had no private confession, there was only a public confession. When someone felt that he had become alien to the Church by what he was or what he did, he came to the meeting of the Christians and in the presence of all he said: "This is what I am. Can you accept me as I am and are you prepared to carry me?—because I cannot promise, simply because I renounce inwardly my past, to be able to live up to this change of heart." And then it was for the congregation to say: "Yes, we give you gratuitously our trust, we will support you, we will carry you. You come back to us whenever you stumble or slip. We make ourselves responsible for you, not because we are superior, better than you, but because we are one living body of people and if you perish, we all perish, in the same way in which a body that undergoes an amputation is no longer whole." This is so important. It cannot be done in the vastness of Christendom, but it can be done between two or three, perhaps five or ten people who would be prepared to say: "Look, I have hated you all my life," or "Look, this is what I have been hiding from you ever since we have met. Can you help me out?"

I have told several of you on occasion the story of a man in his twenties who came to confession to Father Alexander Elchaninov at one of the Russian Student Christian Movement conferences. He had been an officer during the First World War, during the Civil War; he had become a hardened man, and he said to Father Alexander: "I can confess all my sins before you, but a thing I cannot do is to feel sorry for them. My heart is of stone. I can give you a list of them, tell you that intellectually I reject them, but that is all I can do." And Father Alexander said: "No, don't do that. It will be no use, because unless your heart breaks, unless your heart melts, your confession will give no fruits. I will tell you what to do. When all the conference is gathered together for the Liturgy, before the service begins you'll come forward and you will make your confession in the presence of all those who have gathered here. This is your salvation." And the man accepted the challenge. And before the liturgy he came out and explained what he was about to do. And he began to speak. What he expected was to see people recoil in horror, turn away in disgust, look with coldness. What he saw was people who looked at him with all the compassion they were capable of, all the admiration they had for a man who for the sake of integrity and resurrection, his own, could speak such truth in their presence. And seeing these open hearts, seeing the way he was listened to with reverence, with awe, he burst into tears, and he could make his confession, and his heart melted.

This is an example of what should be possible in our midst. It is not. You could not possibly do that in a parish at large. But again and again I say: we can to do it with one another, to one another, in groups. I do not mean to have special groups of people who pour out their souls to one another. But there *must* be in our midst this possibility. And then the pseudo-community, which we *are*, of people who are well protected against each other and well protected even against themselves, could become an incipient community at least. You know, what happens to us when we protect ourselves is something that happens to the corals. The corals are very frail organisms that live in the sea. They are so frail that for their defense they secrete a shell, this beautiful coral-colored shell, and they are safe within it until, soon, they die, because what they needed was the water that surrounded them, but this water was both their food, their milieu, but also full of danger, their death. And they chose protection, and they died of it.

And this happens to all of us to a certain degree. We must accept to become vulnerable; we must accept to be both judged and saved; we must accept one another. Saint Paul says: "Receive one another as Christ has received you." How does he receive us? He receives us as we are, not conditionally. He receives us simply because we come to him, and when we do not come. *He* comes to us, not claiming our confidence, but being there until we feel we can speak to him. Openness means to be vulnerable, and this can be done only if we *want*, desperately, to reach wholeness and integrity. We can be such beautiful massifs of corals, and people would look and say: "What a forest of corals and how beautiful they are!" And they are dead. This they will not say, because they will see only the exterior. And this is a problem in each human community, but in the Church it is a problem that stands before us as an absolute challenge, because unless we attempt to achieve it, we have failed in becoming the Church singly and collectively. Of all people I am probably the worst in that respect, because I am a lone wolf by character. I have been trained to be alone to function. I am aware of that. But we must try.

I will end at this point my talk. Think about it—whether it makes any sense—and then next time I will try to go deeper into this question of how we can, from being a pseudo-community, harmonious, glib, well-behaved, become a *community*, have a common life, a real human life within us, and the life of God within us.

Let Us Build Together

*Nietzsche once said, "One must carry a chaos within oneself if one wishes
to give birth to a star." . . . There is in the writings of Saint Hermas, . . .
a vision: he sees the angels of God building the city of God . . . and he sees
that they choose square stones with sharp edges. . . . And then there are
stones that seem so beautiful in their material, so smooth in their shape—
round, oval—and they are rejected. Because it is only those stones that
can be fitted together and cemented together that can be used for the
building of these walls of the Heavenly Jerusalem.*

~: 9 :~

Achieving an Ideal

JUNE 28, 1990

*T*HIS IS THE LAST IN THE SERIES OF TALKS, WHICH I have chosen to give on churchianity versus Christianity. The aim was to look at the ideal that is offered us by Christ and in Christ, which is revealed to us also in the lives of the saints, and to contrast it with the way we live. Of course we cannot live up to the saintliness of the great heroes of the spirit—although Christ says to us "I give you an example for you to follow," we imagine that we can be an adequate image of him; but rather, in more than one way, when collectively or individually we do not correspond to the ideal that is offered us, it is not because of our weakness or our imperfection, but because we made the wrong choices; because we aimed at something that is less than our glory; because we tried to build a society that is less than the Church.

And this is why I insisted so heavily on what makes us so different from the ideal we proclaim. It is good that we are aware of this ideal. It is good that we proclaim it as perfectly as we can, with the greatest possible wholeness and integrity and beauty. But then we must do all that depends on us to achieve it, and achieving an ideal is always a very costly thing. It is not in vain that Christ says, "If anyone wishes to follow me, let him renounce himself, let him turn away from himself, let him forget the exclusive interest that he has in himself. Let him look beyond himself, let him look

God-wards, let him look at me." Let him look at those people who have been faithful to our Lord, who took up their cross and walked step after step in the footsteps of the incarnate God. Let us look at people around us and see them with new eyes, with eyes that are capable of discerning good and evil. And let us build together—not a society of men that is more livable, perhaps, than societies that have been attempted in the past, but a society that is perhaps eternal, a society in the making, a society that may at times be chaotic, but one that has wholeness. The German writer Nietzsche once said, "One must carry a chaos within oneself if one wishes to give birth to a star." This applies not to individuals alone, perhaps less to individuals than to societies, to groups of people.

I spoke last time of the false community that we are, which all communities are to a greater or lesser extent, communities that are characterized by the fact that everyone does all he can or she can not to be wounded and therefore locks himself or herself up. There is a self-being that we do not disclose to ourselves or to one another, either for better or worse, and we cannot communicate with one another. We are well protected, we are hard, we are like crustaceans. There may be immense frailty inside, but it is inaccessible from the outside. But this is not all there is to it. In a false community everyone protects himself against everyone else. Everyone tries not to be known, except in ways he or she chooses. Everyone tries to work out ways in which all relationships will be smooth. This is not community.

There is in the writings of Saint Hermas, one of the seventy disciples of Christ, a vision: he sees the angels of God building the city of God, the new Jerusalem, and he sees that they choose square stones with sharp edges and place them next to one another, cementing them together. And then there are stones that seem so beautiful in their material, so smooth in their shape—round, oval—and they are rejected. Because it is only those stones that can be fitted together and cemented together that can be used for the building of these walls of the Heavenly Jerusalem. And when we try to create a society in which every one of us is safe from the other, are we not creating a society of people who are like smooth, rounded stones that can in no way be fitted together with others? What is needed then is a hammer that will break the smoothness and reshape them.

But this is only one side of the problem. There is another side. No one of us is capable of enduring this complete solitude. No one is capable of being locked into himself. No one of us is capable of not seeing in others those features that frighten and cause us to shut ourselves in. And so suspiciousness grows, fear grows, dislike develops, hatreds appear. And this cannot be contained within one person or another. It must have expression one way or another. The true expression is given us by Christ in the gospel: "If you have aught against your brother, go and tell him. If he refuses to listen, speak to him in the presence of two or three witnesses; if then again he pays no heed to your words, tell the whole community. And if he then refuses to listen, then only, but only then, let him become to you a stranger."

This is the way in which we may break through our fears, our suspicions, our dislikes, our hatreds. But instead of this the false community has developed other methods of getting these various emotions off one's chest. They may be simply evil: it is gossip, it is slander. When a few people who have a grudge—or a dislike or hatred—against another person, crowd together to say all that they are not in a position to say to this person face to face or in presence of witnesses. Gossip around us arises, slander develops, and divisions increase, because around every person who has aught against anyone, a nucleus of people forms who share in that attitude. And then there is perhaps a more monstrous way of acting, a "pious" way in which slander assumes a mask of piety, in which a person says to another, "I know how much you love so and so, respect so and so, and yet I have discovered something evil about him or her; and I want you to pray for this person. And then comes the description—the flood of all the evil that has accumulated in the mind and heart of the other person." And [it is through] the door of "compassion," of piety, of brotherliness that evil becomes rampant.

[...] I have spoken of the book in which [M.] Scott Peck describes a small monastic community that was dying out, and that remark made by a rabbi to the superior, who was sharing with him his agony about the community: "I don't know what you should do about it, but I can tell you one thing for sure: one of the five of you who remain is the Messiah." And then, the story goes, each of them began to ask himself a question: "Is this brother, that brother of mine, the Messiah whom I am incapable of recognizing? Could I possibly be the Messiah?" And the result was that each of these five brethren began to look at one another with new eyes, treat one another as the *possible* Messiah, and behave also, each of them, as though *they* were the possible Messiah. And the whole situation changed. A relationship grew between them that had never been there before. They were not unaware of what was wrong in themselves or in others; only they wondered: "Is it possible that despite all such and such characteristics, which I see so obviously, my brother can be God's anointed one, the one that saved my soul."

If we could look at one another in this spirit. Oh, we can of course, do that easily when we are away from each other, we can do that easily when theoretically we know that each of us is made in the image of God, that this image is imprinted deeply in everyone's soul, that if I do not see it, it is because it is partly distorted, partly defaced, and partly hidden. But I can believe that it is there, as I can believe, strange though it may sound to me, that I also have in me the image of God. But this is something that we can do theoretically. There are other things that we must do actively. Just because we know it, theoretically, it does not teach us in fact, in actual fact, to act toward one another as though we were icons of Christ.

Can you imagine what would happen if we were given an icon, badly damaged, desecrated? We would take it in our hands with both a deep sense of reverence and a deep sense of compassion. We would look with a sense of horror at the damage and with a sense of awe at what remains of the holy face of God. There are moments when we can do that concerning one another. There are moments when we are at peace, in a strange peace that God can give, which nothing else can give. And then we become unaware of ourselves and can see another person, and see both the damage and the beauty—the little, perhaps, of what is left of the glory—and the darkness. And instead of judging, condemning, hating the darkness, we feel a deep compassion. This happens, I think, to every priest who hears a confession. This happens when someone opens his or her heart to another person, and when they discover that apart from the ugliness there is suffering, there is pain, there is agony of mind—not agony of mind concerning the circumstances of one's life, but agony of mind about being as we are, being as I am.

If we could look at one another and see that in the darkness there is a flicker of light, and that the person who is plunged into this darkness cries desperately, that he longs desperately for this flicker of light to extend, to pervade the darkness, to annihilate it, we would then hear the cry of agony much more loudly than we see the darkness itself. If we only could realize that there is no evil in a person that is not at the same time a suffering in this person. Not, perhaps, the kind of suffering that we would like to see in this person—repentance, broken-heartedness, humility—but the pain and the suffering and the agony of a person who feels that he or she is drowning in evil and does not know how to save himself or herself. We could at times see this better if we were determined to see, but we are not determined to see. And this is why churchianity overwhelms Christianity. This is where what is pagan in us speaks louder than what is Christ in us.

And so there are two sides in this process. We are told that we should not judge, but we are not told that we should not assess things. We are not told to confuse good and evil, light and darkness, truth and untruth, and so forth. We are called, to use the words of Saint Paul, to learn to discern the spirits, to look at situations and see them not for what they are visibly, ostensibly, but see them as God sees them. This is a curious thing about the Old Testament: it is a history of mankind written, not from the point of view of a historian, not from the point of view of a human onlooker or scholar. It is a history of mankind written as God sees it. And there are passages that are so puzzling: king so-and-so lived and reigned twenty-six years, and in his time the Jews began to worship on the hills, and the punishment of God came upon the nations. What is the logic of such a statement? Is there nothing in twenty-six years of reign to be mentioned except this triviality of the place where the Jews worshipped? And why has punishment come? Simply because in these twenty-six years the Jews had begun to worship in a pagan way on the summit of the hills, and the king had allowed them to fall away from the true faith into the faith of the heathen, and it was the end.

If we could look at one another and at ourselves in the same spirit; if we could look at one another, to the extent we can—and we can to a very great extent—as God looks, and assess evil where there is evil, and not, in the name of false charity and false Christianity, shut our eyes to it, and certainly not call good what is simply evil, but at the same time if we could see evil as the greatest misery that can wound a person, that can come upon a person—that to be sinful, to be evil in one way or another, to one degree or another, is the greatest tragedy—then we would be able to see evil with compassion, to see evil with the desire to help this person, and not to reject. We would see that our task is to help and to heal, not to turn away like the Levite or the priest who passed by the man who had fallen into the hands of the robbers on the way from Jerusalem to Jericho.

But then there are two sides to the problem. On the one hand, we must be prepared to open ourselves and be seen, and this may be a very frightening thing. And I am not speaking of being seen in the sense of other people seeing the bad actions, the evil actions of our life, but the ugliness of our face, the degree to which the image of God has not only been simply distorted, but has become a caricature in us. And the other thing is the readiness to look and to accept. It is accepting on both sides to be vulnerable, to be wounded very deeply by what we see, and be wounded very deeply by being seen. Are we prepared for that? It is only if we are prepared for all these complex emotions that we can gradually break through to one another, break through and meet—meet with the sense of awe, meet with the sense of horror, meet with the sense of compassion, meet with tears of shame and tears of pity. To what extent are we capable of this?—willing, prepared for this? This is the main question that we must ask ourselves. It may be done at times in a small circle of people who already trust one another. It may be the family, it may be a small group of friends, it may be any unit of people who have grown to trust one another—who trust one another enough to say, "Look, I will tell you what I am, and I am not what you imagine I am," to someone who would be able to open himself to the wound or disillusionment of horror, of pain, and, at the same time, on both sides to have a sense of deep gratitude. Because the one would be liberated, would be freed from imprisonment, from being a prison of self but also a prison of the blackmail of evil.

This is not possible to do in a wider community, as our community is. It is sad, but we cannot trust one another at large. We cannot trust that every one of us will listen to someone's confession with compassion, with broken-heartedness, with reverence, with prayer, with readiness to carry the other person's burden unto salvation, indeed, to carry the other person as the good shepherd carries the lost sheep, or as the Savior carries the cross. It may be sufficient: Simon of Cyrene helped Christ carry his cross, but it is Christ who brought it to Calvary, and on Calvary Christ had to die upon it. This is also something that is within the *possible*. It may terrify us if we imagine that we would have to do this alone, but it is not alone that we will do it.

There is a story about two martyrs of North Africa [Perpetua and Felicity]. They were in prison. One of them [Felicity] was pregnant, and the time came for her to give birth to her child, and she cried and wailed. And the guard of the prison laughed at her and said, "Look at the misery you are in for a thing as natural as childbirth. What will you do when beasts tear you apart in the circus?" And the saint said to him, "I am now suffering natural suffering, but when I will be in the circus, Christ will be in me." And indeed, she died the serene and tragic death of the martyr. In her the words of Saint Paul came true that "all things are possible unto me in the power of Christ who sustains me."

So we could begin to create cells of true community within our wider community, not by huddling together among people who are already akin to one another, but also including people we find difficult. Not the people whom we cannot carry, but people whose burden we feel we could *attempt* to carry—open ourselves and allow another to open himself, while we suspend judgment. When things become too difficult, too terrifying, say—"Look, stop. I can't endure more. Let me live with what you have already disclosed to me. Let me pray about it. Let me try to learn and accept what I now know about you without disclosing to me more that I can't." And it would apply also to the other one saying, "I will tell you as much as I can, not everything. Because I'm still afraid—afraid of you, afraid of rejection, afraid of increasing alienation, afraid of increasing solitude and loneliness, afraid of creating contempt and hatred where there was only simple indifference." It is a difficult process.

But then what is our ideal? It is an ideal identified once in a small leaflet by Professor Zander called *The Social Implications of the Doctrine of the Holy Trinity*, where he said that the Holy Trinity is the perfect image of what a society should be: three persons, each of them united to each other without intrusion, without rejection. The problem of the third one is a touchstone of the community. Can we accept the third one?

And so, in this last talk what I would like to say as a conclusion is that I have tried to present to you various aspects of our Church life that are legitimate, but that, instead of being an expression, full of beauty, of the life, the common life of the Church, have become self-sufficient. The divine beauty that is revealed to us becomes mere aesthetics, rules of life that are commandments of life—ways in which one can live—become rules that kill life. And communities are all too often smooth because there is no acceptance and no rejection of one another, only mutual protection against each other, and self-protection. I have spoken so often of the Holy Trinity, reminding you of what Saint Gregory of Nazianzus says: that God is three persons, because only three persons can be an image of perfect love, or of the exaltation of oneness and a total readiness to lay down one's life—the cross and the resurrection, simultaneously because a moment comes when the cross is the sign of victory, not the instrument of defeat.

So what I suggest—to myself, to all of you: let us make an attempt at, if not achieving, at least at attempting the kind of relationship out of which a community can develop. How beautiful it would be if, beginning with small nuclei, with small groups of two or three, the barriers of estrangement, of rejection, of fear, of hatred, of indifference could gradually melt or be broken through—how beautiful if we accepted to be vulnerable so that we should not be frightening, if we accepted to be open, to receive and to give—in truth. If we think of the Church as an organism, simultaneously and equally human and divine, in which the fullness of God abides and *all* that is human is in the making. If we could think of ourselves as limbs of one body, the destiny of which depends on the destiny of *each*. If we realized that no one of us can hope to be saved without the others—how creative our community could be!

Well, this is all I wanted to say on the subject. The meeting is about to end. Shall we be quiet a few moments, and then pray:

"O Lord, I know not what to ask of thee. Thou lovest me more than I know how to love even myself. Help me to see my real needs, which are concealed from me. I dare not ask either a cross, or consolation. I can only wait on thee. My heart is open to thee. Visit and help me, for thy great mercy's sake. Strike me and heal me, cast me down and raise me up. I worship in silence thy holy will, thine inscrutable ways. I offer myself as a sacrifice to thee. I put all my trust in thee. I have no other desire than to fulfill thy will. Teach me how to pray. Pray thou thyself in me."

"O Lord, absolve, remit, forgive our transgressions, whether wittingly or unwittingly committed, whether in word, in deed, in thought, whether by day or night, forgive us all. Thou Lord art merciful and thou lovest mankind. Forgive, O Lord, those who hate and wrong us. Do good to those who are doers of good. Grant the petitions of our brethren and sisters in prayers that are for their salvation and eternal life. Visit those who are sick, and heal them; guard those at sea; travel with those who travel; look down in mercy at those who are in prisons; give thy support and guidance to our rulers; to those who help us and are merciful to us grant forgiveness of sins; on those who charge us, unworthy though we are, to pray for them—have mercy, according to thy great mercy."

"Remember, O Lord, our parents, our brethren, our sisters, who have fallen asleep, and give them rest that the light of thy countenance visit them. Remember, O Lord, those who bring forth fruits and do good works in thy holy churches and grant them all their petitions that are from the good of eternal life. Be mindful, O Lord, of those of us who are lonely, sinful, unworthy servants, and lead us into the path of thy commandments, by the prayers of thy merciful Mother and of all thy saints. As thou art blessed from ages to ages. Amen."

"Most glorious ever-virgin Mother of Christ our God, bring our prayers unto thy Son and our God and by thee may he save our souls."

"O Father, thou art my hope, O Son, thou art my refuge, O Holy Spirit, thou art my protection, O Holy Trinity, glory be to thee. Amen."

Index of Names

Andrew of Crete, Saint, was Archbishop of Crete at the end of the seventh century and the beginning of the eighth. He was a true luminary of the Church, a great hierarch—a theologian, teacher, and hymnographer, best known for writing the Great Canon. His feast day is celebrated on July 4.

Angelus Silesius (Johann Scheffler) (1624–1677) was a German Catholic priest and physician, known as a mystic and religious poet. He took holy orders under the Franciscans and was ordained a priest. He composed fifty-five tracts and pamphlets condemning Protestantism. He is now remembered chiefly for his religious poetry: *The Soul's Holy Desires*, a collection of religious hymn texts used by Catholics and Protestants, and *The Cherubinic Wanderer* (Classics of Western Spirituality; ed. Maria Shrady and Josef Schmidt [Paulist Press, 1986]), a collection of short poems.

Anthony the Great, Saint (ca. 254–356), also known as Anthony of Egypt. He was a leader among the Desert Fathers, who were Christian monks in the Egyptian desert in the third and fourth centuries. The Orthodox Church celebrates his feast on January 17.

Anthony of the Kiev Caves, Saint (1983–1073), was one of the founders of the Kiev Pechersk Lavra (Monastery of the Kiev Caves) during the times of Kievan Rus' (AD 1051). This monastery became a major center of Orthodox Christianity in the

Slavic world. His feast day is celebrated September 2, and also on July 10, when an appearance of the Mother of God foretold of his impending death.

Bloy, Léon (1846–1917), was a French novelist, essayist, pamphleteer, poet, critic, polemicist, and a fervent Roman Catholic convert who preached spiritual revival through suffering and poverty. Bloy's works are extremely varied in form, but they reveal a unity of thought: through pain and destitution man is redeemed by the Holy Spirit and is awakened to the hidden language of the universe. His autobiographical novels, *Le Désespéré* (1886, *Despairing*) and *La Femme pauvre* (1897, *The Woman Who Was Poor*), express his mystical conception of woman as the Holy Spirit and of love as a devouring fire.

Bulgakov, Sergei Nikolaevich (1871–1944), was a priest of the Russian Church in the early twentieth century. He was noted as an Orthodox theologian, philosopher, and economist. After an early interest in Marxism, he returned to his religious roots in Orthodox Christianity. He wrote extensively, and after being exiled by the new Communist government of Russia, he became part of the community of Russians in Paris, taking part in the founding of the St Sergius Orthodox Theological Institute in Paris.

Elizabeth of the Trinity (1880–1906) was a French Discalced Carmelite nun, mystic, and spiritual writer. She has been beatified by the Catholic Church.

Elchaninov, Alexander (1881–1934), was ordained a Russian Orthodox priest in France after the Russian Revolution. He also was a Church historian and writer, and one of the leaders of the Russian Student Christian Movement. His book *Diary of a Rus-*

sian Priest (St Vladimir's Seminary Press, 1997 repr.) is truly a spiritual treasure and classic.

Ephrem the Syrian, Saint, was a prolific Syriac language hymn writer and theologian of the fourth century. He is venerated by Christians throughout the world, but especially among Syriac Christians. His feast day in the Orthodox Church is January 28.

Florovsky, Georges Vasilievich (1893–1979), was an Orthodox priest, theologian, historian, and ecumenist. Born in Odessa, in the Russian Empire, he spent his working life in Paris and New York. With Sergei Bulgakov and Vladimir Lossky he was one of the most influential Orthodox Christian theologians of the mid-twentieth century. He was particularly concerned that modern Christian theology might receive inspiration from the intellectual debates of the patristic traditions of the undivided Church rather than from later Scholastic or Reformation categories of thought.

Gillet, Lev (1893–1980), was an archimandrite of the Ecumenical Patriarchate. Brought up in the Roman Catholic tradition, he joined the Orthodox Church and worked for the union of the churches. Principal publications, originally in French (under the pseudonym "A Monk of the Eastern Church"), include *Orthodox Spirituality: An Outline of the Orthodox Ascetical and Mystical Tradition* (St Vladimir's Seminary Press, 1978), *The Year of Grace of the Lord: A Scriptural and Liturgical Commentary on the Calendar of the Orthodox Church* (St Vladimir's Seminary Press, 1980), and *The Jesus Prayer* (St Vladimir's Seminary Press 1987).

de Gobineau, Joseph Arthur Comte (1816–1882), was a French aristocrat, novelist, and man of letters who became famous for developing the theory of the Aryan master race in his book *An*

Essay on the Inequality of the Human Races. De Gobineau is credited as being the father of modern racial demography, and his works are today considered very early examples of scientific racism. Hitler and Nazism borrowed much of Gobineau's ideology, though Gobineau himself was not antisemitic, and may even be characterised as philosemitic.

Grabar, Igor Emmanuilovich (1871–1960), was a Russian post-impressionist painter, publisher, restorer, and historian of art. Grabar, descendant of a wealthy Rusyn family, was trained as a painter by Ilya Repin in Saint Petersburg and by Anton Abe in Munich. In 1910–1915 Grabar edited and published his *opus magnum*, the *History of Russian Art*. The *History* employed the finest artists and critics of the period. Grabar personally wrote the issues on architecture that set an unsurpassed standard of understanding and presenting the subject.

John Chrysostom, Saint (347–407), Archbishop of Constantinople, was a notable Christian bishop and preacher in Syria and Constantinople. He is famous for eloquence in public speaking and his denunciation of abuse of authority in the Church and in the Roman Empire of the time. He was an ardent ascetic. After his death he was named Chrysostom, which comes from the Greek *Chrysostomos,* "golden-mouthed." His feast day in the Orthodox Church is November 13. He is also celebrated among the Three Holy Hierarchs, together with Saints Basil the Great and Gregory the Theologian (January 30).

Gregory of Nyssa, Saint (ca. 335–395), was bishop of Nyssa and a prominent theologian of the fourth century. He was the younger brother of Basil the Great and friend of Gregory the Theologian.

He was an erudite theologian who made significant contributions to the doctrine of the Trinity and the Nicene Creed. He is commemorated on January 10.

Hackel, Sergei Alekseyevich (1931–2005), was senior priest in Britain of the Russian Orthodox Diocese of Sourozh, combining his BBC World Service work with the duties of a parish priest in Lewes, Sussex, and with lecturing in Russian at Sussex University. His literary work consisted mainly of articles rather than books, but his fine life of Mother Maria Skobtsova, who died in the Nazi Ravensbrück concentration camp (*Pearl Of Great Price*, 1965; published by St Vladimir's Seminary Press in 1981), propelled Mother Maria into the public spotlight. A believer in ecumenism, for thirty years he was editor of *Sobornost'*, the journal of the Orthodox-Anglican Fellowship of St Alban and St Sergius.

Hermas, Apostle, Saint, was one of the Seventy Apostles and bishop in Philipopoulis. The Shepherd of Hermas is also traditionally ascribed to him. He is referenced in Romans 16.14, and his feast day is celebrated on May 31 and November 5, and on January 4 among the Seventy.

Irenaeus of Lyons, Saint (ca.130–202), was bishop of Lugdunum in Gaul, which is now Lyons, France. He was an early Church Father and apologist, and his writings were formative in the early development of Christian theology. He was a disciple of St Polycarp of Smyrna, who himself was a disciple of the Apostle John the Theologian. His feast day is August 23.

Lewis, Clive Staples (1898–1963), commonly called C. S. Lewis, was a novelist, poet, academic, medievalist, literary critic, essayist, lay theologian, and Christian apologist. Born in Belfast, Ireland, he held academic positions at both Oxford University and Cambridge University. He is best known both for his fictional work, especially *The Screwtape Letters*, *The Chronicles of Narnia*, and *The Space Trilogy*, and for his nonfiction Christian apologetics, such as *Mere Christianity*, *Miracles*, and *The Problem of Pain*.

Macarius the Great, Saint (295–392), also known as Macarius the Egyptian, was among the most influential Desert Fathers of Egypt, and a disciple of St Anthony the Great. The day appointed for his feast in Eastern Orthodoxy is January 19.

Maximus the Confessor, Saint (ca. 580–662), was a monk and ascetical writer known especially for his courageous fight against the heresy of Monothelitism. His feast day in the Church is celebrated on January 21.

Maimonides, Moses (1135–1204), was a preeminent medieval Spanish, Sephardic Jewish philosopher, astronomer, and one of the most prolific and influential Torah scholars and physicians of the Middle Ages. He was posthumously acknowledged to be one of the foremost rabbinical arbiters and philosophers in Jewish history. He was known as a rabbi, physician, and philosopher in Morocco and Egypt.

van der Mensbrugghe, Alexis (1899–1980), was a Roman Catholic Benedictine monk convert to Orthodox Christianity who worked to establish a Gallican liturgical rite as an archbishop of the Church of Russia.

Mochulski, Konstantin Vasilievich (1892–1948), Russian literary critic, theologian, one of the leading figures of the Russian Orthodox emigrés movement. He taught in universities of St

Petersburg, Sofia, Sorbonne, and St Sergius in Paris. Konstantin Mochulsky's critical biography of F. M. Dostoevsky is, in the words of George Gibian, the "best single work in any language about Dostoevsky's work as a whole."

Moffatt, James (1870–1944), was a theologian and graduate of Glasgow University. Moffatt trained at the Free Church College, Glasgow, and was a practicing minister before becoming Professor of Greek and New Testament Exegesis at Mansfield College, Oxford. Later he was Washburn Professor of Church History at the Union Theological Seminary, New York. He wrote one of the standard Modern English Bible translations, the *Moffatt New Translation (MNT)*.

Nietzsche, Friedrich Wilhelm (1844–1900), was a German philosopher, cultural critic, poet, composer, and Latin and Greek scholar. He wrote several critical texts on religion, morality, contemporary culture, philosophy, and science.

Pascal, Blaise (1623–1662), was a French mathematician, physicist, inventor, writer, and Christian philosopher. Pascal's earliest work was in the natural and applied sciences where he made important contributions to the study of fluids, and clarified the concepts of pressure and vacuum. Pascal also wrote in defense of the scientific method.

Peck, Morgan Scott (1936–2005), was an American psychiatrist and bestselling author, best known for his first book, *The Road Less Traveled*, published in 1978 and more recently by Touchstone in 2003.

Samarin, Yuri Fyodorovich (1819–1876), was a leading Russian Slavophile thinker and one of the architects of the Emancipation reform of 1861. He came to believe that "Orthodoxy, and Orthodoxy alone, is a religion that philosophy can recognize," and that "the Orthodox Church cannot exist apart from Hegel's philosophy." In his latter years, Samarin continued to write copiously on national and "peasant" questions, advocating the step-by-step abolition of serfdom.

Seraphim of Sarov, Saint (1754–1833), is one of the most renowned Russian monks and mystics in the Eastern Orthodox Church. He is generally considered the greatest of the nineteenth-century *startsty* (plural of *starets,* elder). He taught that the purpose of the Christian life was to acquire the Holy Spirit. Perhaps his most popular quotation is, "Acquire a peaceful spirit, and thousands around you will be saved." His biographer Nicholas Motovilov was one of his "spiritual children." In one account, he describes the miraculous transfiguration of the starets' face.

Symeon the New Theologian, Saint (949–1022), was a monk and poet who was one of three saints canonized by the Eastern Orthodox Church and given the title of "Theologian" (along with John the Apostle and Gregory of Nazianzus). "Theologian" was not applied to Symeon in the modern academic sense of theological study, but to recognize someone who spoke from personal experience of the vision of God. One of his principal teachings was that humans could and should experience *theoria* (literally "contemplation," or direct experience of God). His feast day is celebrated on October 12.

Tikhon of Zadonsk, Saint (1724–1783), was a Russian Orthodox bishop and spiritual writer. He retired to the monastery of Zadonsk and lived there until he died. His relics were kept there and, after many reports of miracles that occurred around them, he was canonized as a saint. He is remembered by many as the "Russian Chrysostom." His feast day is celebrated on August 13.

Theokritoff, Vladimir (1881–1950), the priest of the Parish of the Dormition of the Mother of God in London in the 1940s. Under him, the parish moved to the Moscow Patriarchate, believing that this decision would help support the suffering Church in Russia. Soon afterwards Fr Vladimir died. He was followed by a young priest, who had originally come to England from Paris to the Fellowship of St Alban and St Sergius. His name was Anthony Bloom, the future Metropolitan Anthony of Sourozh.

Theodosius of the Kiev Caves, Saint (1009—1074), along with St Anthony, is considered to be a founder in the eleventh century of the Kiev Pechersk Lavra (Monastery of the Kiev Caves) and of monasticism in Russia. He brought cenobitic monasticism to Kievan Rus'. His feast day is May 3.

Zander, Lev Alexandrovich (1893–1964), a Russian philosopher, one of the leaders of the International Ecumenical Movement. The publication (*Les implications sociales de la doctrine de la Trinity* [Paris, 1936], 23 pp.), mentioned by Met. Anthony, was actually written by Valentina Alexandrovna Zander, wife of Prof. Zander.